And God Chose Dreams

To Elevate Our Mind and Thoughts During Times of Change

Michael L. Mathews

AuthorHouse™
1663 Liberty Drive, Suite 200
Bloomington, IN 47403
www.authorhouse.com
Phone: 1-800-839-8640

©*2008 Michael L. Mathews. All rights reserved.*
No part of this book may be reproduced, stored in a retrieval system, or transmitted by any means without the written permission of the author.
First published by AuthorHouse 12/19/2008

ISBN: 978-1-4389-3381-8 (sc)

Printed in the United States of America
Bloomington, Indiana
This book is printed on acid-free paper.

Table of Contents

Dedication and Special Thanks 1
Foreword.. 3
Preface 5
Introduction.. 9
Chapter One ....
    Why Dreams Are Increasing 13
    1. Our Minds and Thoughts Are Saturated 15
    2. Dreams Allow Us to Align Our Thoughts with God's Thoughts 19
    3. God Stated That Dreams Would Increase in the Last Days 23
    4. Personalizing His Message... 26

Chapter Two ....
    Biblical Dreams from the Old Testament..............................35

Chapter Three ....
    Biblical Dreams and Visions from the New Testament 91

Chapter Four ....
    Application and Interpretation of Dreams 127
    Overview of Applying Dreams for Application Today......... 128
    Should Dreams Be Taken More Seriously?......................... 133

Chapter Five ....
    Scientifically Speaking 147
    The Basics of Sleep and Dream Cycles............................... 148
    The Recent History of Dream Understanding 151
    REM (Paradoxical) Sleep 152
    Lucid Dreaming... 152
    Modern-Day Examples Where Dreams Helped Society.... 153

A View of Dreams by Carl Jung 156
Dream Recall 157
Frequently Asked Questions About Dreams 158

Chapter Six ....
Samples of Dreams and Interpretation 163

Chapter Seven ....
Summary 177
Bibliography 183
Notes and Contact Information 185
Important Take Aways By Reader 187

Dedication and Special Thanks

First, I would like to thank God for the patience He has shown during the past seventeen years, by developing my life in a fuller manner. At first it appeared to be an awkward method, but after seventeen years He has proven that not only is He faithful, but a masterful builder who molds a person individually, and in a very thoughtful pattern to produce something a person could never do by themselves.

> *"But Christ is faithful as a son over God's house. And we are His house, if we hold on to our courage and hope of which we boast."*
> Hebrews 3:6 (NIV)

Secondly, this book would not be possible without the cooperation in ministry of my beautiful wife and partner, Pam. She has been a true encourager and partner in God's work. She has filled a place in my heart and life that no other person could have filled. Together, God has allowed us to produce the outcome of this book and many other miraculous endeavors that have exceeded our greatest expectations. All of my work with other ministers and coworkers combined cannot compare to the teamwork we have built together. God has built this house that we share in our hearts!

Thirdly, without the life and joy of my two daughters, Jessica and Tiffany, this author would have never seen the beauty of life and dreams that made the beginning of any endeavor possible. Thank you Jessica and Tiffany!

— *Michael L. Mathews* —

Last but not least, I am indebted to Glenn Gohr, reference archivist for the Heritage Center at the Assemblies of God Headquarters, Springfield, Missouri, for utilizing his English, editing, and research capabilities to make the book more readable.

FOREWORD

Michael and I began our professional relationship 10-years ago when we worked together in the early years of the internet to develop and teach the first internet-based ministerial courses offered through Global University, a distance education learning school of the Assemblies of God. Without a doubt, Michael is well-versed in Scripture and applies it in practical everyday ways to everyday people. In this volume, he has done a great service to the Church by dealing with a subject which in the past has only been dealt with by scholars interpreting the Scriptures. But if dreams and visions were such an integral part of the biblical narrative, and if God has promised that in the last days men and women would dream dreams, then shouldn't this important truth be emphasized and taught for the Church today?

Skeptics may ask, "Are dreams and visions really from the Lord? Or are they just a figment of the imagination? Does God speak to people today through dreams and visions? Or is it just a phenomenon of the past that He did when the Scriptures were being written?" From studying Scripture and knowing that God is the same "yesterday and today and forever," I must conclude that God does speak to His Church today through visions and dreams.

One of the many incidents that Michael illuminates in this book is my favorite Bible story — the story of Joseph the dreamer as recorded in Genesis chapters 37-50. Joseph stands out because he had a close walk with God. God spoke to him through spiritual dreams (Gen. 37:6-11), and he was able to interpret the dreams of others (the cupbearer and the baker, as well as Pharaoh). Each dream that God gave to Joseph came true.

I believe that God also speaks to us today through dreams and visions even as he did to Joseph, Ezekiel, Daniel, Peter, John, and others in the Bible. This is prophesied in Joel 2:28-29: "And it shall come to pass afterward, that I will pour out my spirit upon all flesh; and your sons and your daughters shall prophesy, your old men shall dream dreams, your young men shall see visions: And also upon the servants and upon the handmaids in those days will I pour out my spirit" (KJV).

The events of the last days are upon us as foretold by Jesus in Matthew 24 as well as in a multitude of other Scriptures. And the prophecies in Joel and in Acts 2:17 regarding mankind having dreams and visions are coming to pass also. God is still alive, and He still speaks to His Church today. And if He can speak to important Bible figures like Joseph, then we should be willing to follow their examples. We need to have a close walk with God and be open to His leadings, no matter which avenue God may choose to speak to us. I strongly urge you to read *And God Chose Dreams*. It has the potential to revolutionize your life and to bring you into a closer relationship with Christ. I highly recommend this book.

Glenn W. Gohr
Reference Archivist for the Assemblies of God
Springfield, Missouri

PREFACE

Dreams are illustrations from the book your soul is writing about you. ~ Marsha Norman

For God may speak in one way, or in another, yet man does not perceive it. In a dream, in a vision of the night, when deep sleep falls upon men, while slumbering on their beds, then He opens the ears of men, and seals their instruction. In order to turn man from his deed, and conceal pride from man, He keeps back his soul from the Pit, and his life from perishing by the sword.

~ Job 33:14-18 (NKJV)

I am sure the book title, "And God Chose Dreams," caught your attention because you have been experiencing more dreams lately. Am I right? I have surveyed numerous people and found that I am able to quickly grab their attention by asking the question, *"Have you had any dreams or visions lately?"* Each person was immediately drawn into my question and surprised by my asking them this question. I have been asking this specific question because I realize the timeframe we are living in aligns with scriptural evidence that people will be having more dreams and visions.

The majority of the people I have surveyed have all stated they have recently had very specific, repeatable, and/or vivid dreams. A small percentage of the people I asked could not remember any dreams, but came back to me within days and stated that they had a dream since I asked them. All the people that I asked and/or that came back to me inquired how I knew they were having or going to have a dream. I started sharing with them the scriptural evidence that in the last days of the Church Age people would begin to dream more frequently. The next step with these individuals was to share more of the gospel and what God's Word states about dreams. This recent activity has allowed me to share more of God's Word with people who have been drawn into my explanation of Scripture, which was personalized for them. I have never witnessed such a great means to begin to personalize the gospel.

After my informal study, I started asking many more people, including my wife and children, if they have been having dreams on a regular basis. I stand amazed that this simple question has allowed me to experience some of the greatest talks with my daughters, and others, simply based on their dreams and how personal they were to them. It is as if people are waiting for someone to ask them what is happening inside their heart and mind. Possibly God has a reason for this, and thus He chose dreams!

I have found myself sharing with people that dreams are more normal in our present day than most people can comprehend. I share with them that dreaming has been a powerful activity throughout history and so recorded in Scripture. In fact Scripture shares the word "dream" over 165 times. Before I start telling them about the great men and women in Scripture who dreamed, I share the following two powerful evidences that help put their mind at ease: 1) Acts 2:17 states *"And in the last days it will be, God says, that I will pour out my Spirit on all people, and your sons and your daughters will prophesy, and your young men will see visions, and your old men will dream dreams"* (NET Bible). And 2) Daniel 12:4 states *"But you, Daniel, close up these words and seal the book until the time of the end. Many will dash about, and knowledge will increase"* (NET Bible). People generally have responded with one of two replies: 1) That's right; I forgot that Scripture states this, or 2) Wow, I never knew that, but it makes sense now that you mention it.

The passage in Daniel 12:4 is interesting as Daniel was having dreams and visions prior to God making the statement that he was to seal up the dreams (words) until the end of the time. This indicates that the dreams would be revealed and shared when we reach the end of time. We may not be at the very end of time, but we are closer than ever before; therefore dreams should be expected and anticipated as a sign that we are nearing the end.

I have often wondered if God uses dreams in our present day to help get our attention. We are so busy most of the time, that perhaps God whispers in our ears while we are sleeping. This way we can't put him off for another day. In fact, later on in the book you will learn that dreams are exactly that — God's way of whispering in our ear to help and guide us. What an amazing God!!

I understand there are many naysayers reading this who are worried that dreams are spooky and could be influenced by Satan, or last night's pizza talking. Let me challenge you by reminding you that God's Word does not lie! Also, people should be concerned with the weirdo stuff their kids and spouses are viewing on the internet and television, versus God's whispers in their ears. It is completely healthy to encourage your children, spouse, friends, relatives, and other to process their dreams. We should all be reminded that when the great people in Scripture dreamed, it was a time of change, a time to warn them, or a time to provide a new direction. The Apostle Peter's dream/vision on a housetop literally changed religion for all of us. God told Peter that the dream was intended for him to know that Gentiles would be accepted into the plan of salvation (Acts chapter 10).

I believe that God literally wants the worshippers to arise and enjoy His words, His signs, His wonders, and His spiritual gifts in the last days. As we approach the end days we will see the manifestation of God's gifts overshadow the human talents in the church. Talents can't compare to God's gifts and dreams. I pray that leaders would encourage their people to enjoy, embrace, anticipate, and exercise their gifts and dreams at least half as much as they encourage them to exercise their talents, as God is pleased when we use His gifts and do not rely on mere human talent.

Happy reading and dreaming!!

Dreams are like letters from God.
Isn't it time
you answered your mail?
~ Marie-Louise von Franz ~

INTRODUCTION

Sometimes, there's so much thrown at us in the workplace that it's hard to see through the smoke and mirrors. The only time we do that is when we dream.

~ Joshua Estrin

The angelic messenger who had been speaking with me then returned and woke me, as a person is wakened from sleep.

~Zechariah 4:1

Dreams are emerging into a greater percentage of people's lives. On the surface, dreams have a special mystique about them which cause people to generally err on the side of ignoring them or mistaking them as just another unconscious or weird thought. Dreams, however, have a special purpose which generally causes people to do a "double-take," or take a closer look at something that has occurred or is occurring in their life.

More than likely you have purchased this book because you have been having dreams, or have an interest to know if you should be taking your dreams more serious, versus ignoring them. Let me assure you that most dreams are very significant and fulfill a purpose, especially in the day and age in which we live. Yes there are some weird dreams that are merely passing or fleeting thoughts, but generally speaking, what you are dreaming in the present day in which we live has significance for your life. Your very dreams may be able to help you deal with the circumstances you go through and cause you to be more cautious with some of the things that have caused problems in your life.

Dreams are given throughout Scripture to help protect, direct, and provide for individuals, societies, and nations. Any Bible-believing person would be hard pressed to refute the scriptural fact and reality that dreams have historically shaped nations and people. Unfortunately, because many religions have ushered out God's presence and replaced it with performance-based religion ... dreams and the supernatural things of God are often shut down, ignored, or dismissed as not being for today. The fact that they have been shut out does not negate the fact that dreams are real and useful. In chapters two and three you will sense the serious nature of dreams by hearing directly from Scripture on exactly what the Bible teaches about dreams. I would encourage you to jump ahead to chapter two if you are in doubt about the biblical nature of dreams. However, I encourage you to methodically progress through the book and get ready to grab hold of your dreams.

The reason people love to dream and/or are so intrigued by dreams is the reality that dreams provide what some people might see as the ultimate virtual reality experience, where there is no limit to visual empowerment, computational power or memory storage, and even memory recall. In many dreams, where the world exposes itself to the desires of the dreamer, adventure and intrigue are almost guaranteed because the usual laws of physics and of society no longer apply, and many of the apparent mind blocks defined around age, sex, race or religion simply don't apply. In dreams we can be the hero of our own adventure, find romance, fly, travel through "solid" objects, breathe underwater, and perform feats free from embarrassment, peer pressure, monetary limits, and even physical handicaps. The boundaries of imagination that is uncontrolled are the dreamer's only limit. This is the reason some dreams are refreshing and invigorating and others completely exhausting.

It is incredibly amazing why so many people ignore their dream lives when their dream life is real and becoming more active. When you stop and consider the fact that God told people to *"Love the Lord their God with all your heart, mind and soul,"* He meant all aspects of the mind — including the dream aspect of the mind. Surely if I am to serve God with all my mind, I should have some understanding of what is happening in the nighttime hours when my mind is engaged in the deep recess of dreams. It is a shame to see more people intentionally surrender their minds and thoughts in movies, books and music and leave to chance their minds in the dream world, which was created by God. If God is speaking through dreams, then I should take to heart what is being communicated in my mind. What if we believed that God could expand our virtual world, imagination, mind, and desires if we would step beyond our beliefs that God controls our minds — when we surrender them to him? God chose dreams to allow the human mind to be expanded beyond the boundaries that our daily lives live within and fear during the daytime; He literally wants us to catch glimpses of His plans through us.

It is the intent of this book to help bridge three realities about dreams to allow people to relax and enjoy the very nature of their dreams: 1) God used dreams throughout Scripture to guide and help people; 2) God stated that not only did He use dreams, but that He will increase them in the last days before His return; and 3) People everywhere are personally experiencing dreams and visions.

This author's greatest satisfaction will be to hear people state that they have gained a greater appreciation for how vast God is — and how He chose dreams to allow our minds to be expanded during a period of rest (time) when our minds are not limited to the boundaries that we fear and respond to during the day.

> *"And God chose dreams to allow the human mind to be expanded beyond the boundaries that our daily lives live within and fear during the daytime; He literally wants us to catch glimpses of His plans through us."*
>
> ~**Michael L. Mathews**

Chapter One

Why Dreams Are Increasing

> We are so captivated by and entangled in our subjective consciousness that we have forgotten the age-old fact that God speaks chiefly through dreams and visions.
>
> ~ Carl Jung

> And God chose to use dreams to allow the potential for no one to perish and for all of humanity to be without excuse; thus the increase in dreams in the last days.
>
> ~ Michael L. Mathews

The reality that more and more people are dreaming more frequently begs the question as to why? Before we answer the question as to why, we should Scripturally clarify why God chose to use dreams. In Job chapter 13:14-17 God indicates the very nature as to why He uses dreams.

> *For God may speak in one way, or in another, yet man does not perceive it. In a dream, in a vision of the night, when deep sleep falls upon men, while slumbering on their beds, then He opens the ears of men, and seals their instruction. In order to turn man from his deed, and conceal pride from man, He keeps back his soul from the Pit, and his life from perishing by the sword.*
>
> ~ Job 33:14-18 (NKJV)

What an awesome thought to know that God in His infinite wisdom and love chooses to use dreams to whisper into our ears to seal up instruction so we could be prevented from going to hell. This is exactly what the passage is saying. I am so glad to know that this is the intent of God's dreams. Once I have this general rule of thumb as to why God uses dreams, I can measure my dreams and others against them. This rule of thumb really helps when trying to interpret a dream. I personally believe that the frightful nature of most dreams is not from God, but people's personality and "guilt complex" misunderstanding or mistranslating the very essence of the dream God intends to use to help them. Based on this rule of thumb, we can also look back through Scripture and closely examine all dreams and see that God used dreams to help protect people and guide them from going the wrong direction.

Now let's look at the question we started with: *"Why would God decide to increase dreams and visions in the last days?"* There are probably numerous reasons why dreams are increasing that would shed more insight into the simple truth that God stated they would increase. Below I share some of the basic reasons why people are dreaming more than ever before:

1. Our minds and thoughts are completely saturated, and our minds are recalibrating during the evening hours.
2. Dreams and visions allow us to better align our thoughts with God's thoughts.
3. God stated that dreams would increase in the last days, and His Word and fulfillment of His Word cannot be violated. (Matthew 5:18)
4. Dreams are God's personification of the gospel and related information. (Job 33:14-18)

1. Our Minds and Thoughts Are Saturated

The reality of our present day is that we are bombarded with information, questions, decisions, and opinions each and every day. All this information at a macro-level has reached a point that makes it difficult for people to hear, and/or see the subtle choices and decisions required at a micro-level. In fact, God states in his Word that He speaks in a still, small voice. Frequently the daily noise and confusion of life can overshadow God's guidance for us. Just because people have become accustomed to noise and nonstop activity, they assume God speaks through or over all the noise and clamor that occurs in our lives. Oftentimes God is telling us that we need to slow down to a point we will listen and hear His voice. He is not always in the business of shouting over the noise of our life. This does not mean He will not shout over us at times. However, Scripture is clear that God is heard and found by those who set aside time and energy to seek God.

> *A very powerful wind went before the Lord, digging into the mountain and causing landslides, but the Lord was not in the wind. After the windstorm there was an earthquake, but the Lord was not in the earthquake. After the earthquake, there was a fire, but the Lord was not in the fire. After the fire, there was a soft whisper.*
>
> I Kings 19:11-12 (NET Bible)

This may be the very reason God states in the last days He would speak through visions and dreams to young and old alike. At the end of each day when we finally lay down to rest, many of the worries of life settle down and our sub-conscious takes over. Our mind is still in control, but it is acting at a much slower pace that is open to processing things we may have missed during the day. In essence, our brain is recalibrating itself from every event and piece of information it was made to process during the day. This may explain why certain nights we abruptly awake to a reminder of something that we forgot during the day. Our mind is at work, reprocessing or allowing us to process events and circumstances in our everyday life. This in no way implies that every thought or dream is a reprocessing of the day's events. Rather, it is an explanation why dreams often connect with our everyday life, whether from the past, present, or future.

Our minds are very complex and have the potential to process a phenomenal amount of information. However, our minds cannot process all the information at every given point in time when it may be coming at us. God foreknew that the day in which we live would be so perplexing that our minds would need to be recalibrated during the evening hours — thus part of His purpose for increasing dreams in the last days. When sleeping or meditating, our bodies are resting and operating in a more "slow-paced" frame of mind. This slow-paced frame of mind allows us to listen to more of the soft whispers or visuals that we may have heard or seen but were blocked out by the noise or information during the day.

> **"And God chose dreams because he foreknew that the day in which we live would be so perplexing that our minds would need to be recalibrated during the evening hours — thus part of His purpose for increasing dreams in the last days."**
>
> **~ Michael L. Mathews**

This same theory applies to visions as it does to dreams. The only difference according to Scripture between a vision and dream is the implied time and/or place they happen. The Greek word(s) for dream implies a nighttime experience; whereas the Greek word(s) for vision does <u>not</u> imply a nighttime experience. In other words, a vision is like a dream that can happen during the daytime when we are praying or medicating in a means that allows our minds to see things outside the temporal life we operate within. Many people have had visions while praying as their mind was focused on spiritual matters of life. God is in the business of allowing us to see His plans that are generally, if not always at a higher level.

It is essential that we understand that the scientific studies of dreams reveal the reality that dreaming is more normal than abnormal. In addition we need to be reminded of the fact that we have a supernatural God who always desires us to learn, grow and mature into the very people He created us to be. Unfortunately, people often use all the noise of the world to make their decisions and adjustments to their life. The more noise we hear, and the more visual things we see, the more apt we are to make knee-jerk reactions. Let me give you a personal example.

> *I have often stood in front of large crowds and asked them to answer two questions out loud. I start by holding up a piece of white paper and say, "What color is the paper?" They answer, "white!" I then ask, "What do cows drink?" Generally over ninety percent respond with "milk!" But cows drink water! They answered with milk because I just put a visual in front of them to cause a knee-jerk reaction. I then ask the question, "How do you spell shop." They reply "S—H—O—P!" I then proceed to ask the question "What do you do at a green light?" Again about ninety percent say "STOP!" After two or three of these types of questions people realize that they respond in an illogical manner when pieces of other visual information precede the question I am asking. It's amazing … go ahead and try it with a few people. It's amazing how our minds really do work, or should I say don't work?*

All this says is that we have so many things in front of us everyday that we may be wise to process information at a different time, different place, and slower pace, rather than the very place and time we are asked a difficult question. This may be the very reason we have heard so many people faced with a difficult question or decision say … "*Let me sleep on it.*" This phrase has merit, and we use it because we know that after a night of rest we can usually rationalize and think more clearly about difficult decisions. Scientists have proven there is a lot of merit behind this processing of information. One of the reasons being that our minds in sleep are not limited to the same boundaries they are during the day. In sleep our minds have a tendency to process information outside the realm of limitations that we live in during the day! God may very well be leveraging this opportunity at night to allow our religious biases, tradition, and limitations to be blocked so He can expand our minds to a higher level of belief; simply restated, it would be to bring our thoughts up to His thoughts.

Let me play with your mind one step deeper than *"What do cows drink"* to drive home my point about how our minds process data when placed on the spot. Read the paragraph listed below and tell me how many times I used the letter "F" within the paragraph.

The author of this book is trying to focus our minds on the reality of dreams and visions. He of course is making some fabulous points of interest; but I, of course will have to read more before I form an opinion for myself. So far the book provides some good food for thought. Without tipping off the author, I am starting to think this is one of the best books I may have read.

Many people who have read the above paragraph have counted between 10-12 times that I used the letter "F." If you are well below this number, don't worry: read it again. The truth is I used the letter "F" seventeen times in the paragraph above. The answer key to this simple word puzzle is on the last page of this book. Now, you can see that our minds do not process basic information as we perceive it does. Imagine how many more complex answers, decisions, and information our brain is miscalculating and/or seeing without having to go back and reprocess.

Dreams could be increasing simply because on a daily basis the majority of people are receiving such a wider swatch of both binary and visual data that they cannot possibly process it all at that very instant that they receive it. At night our brains kick into gear and try and reprocess the data and/or recalibrate.

2. Dreams Allow Us to Align Our Thoughts with God's Thoughts

In Scripture we find that there are numerous passages that God uses to explain His capabilities versus our limitations and capabilities. In Isaiah 55:8-9 God states that His "thoughts are not your thoughts and [His] ways are not your ways; as far as the heaven is above the earth so are [His] thoughts above your thoughts."

Figure 1 on the next page is an illustration that helps show a few examples of God's capabilities at His level and a few of man's limitations at our level. As you can surmise, there is a huge gap that exists between who God is and who we are without Him.

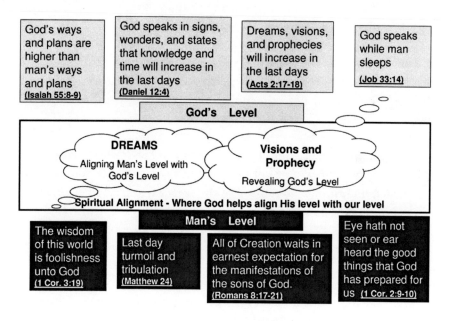

Figure 1 as an illustration –
Aligning Our Plans With God's Plan Through Dreams

The center portion of Figure 1 shows the method that God has often used to get people to see and understand His level. The center piece represents the very thing that God states he would increase in the last day. There is no doubt that man has reverted back to many of his primitive ways in the last few decades; we just hide it under cleaner language that sounds less primitive or sinful. For instance, people have put far more hope in what they can see such as politics and governments, only to realize there was little, if no hope in them. In fact many Americans have recently put far more of their hope in American patriotism, politics, and financial investments only to realize they would have been better off listening to dreams and visions God had spoken to them, and/or through other people.

Let's assume God has always wanted humanity to trust in His ways over man's ways! I believe God is starting to get our attention as He has always wanted you to put more trust in Him than man-made efforts. God's foreknowledge of last day events gave Him the foreknowledge to warn us that He would increase the dreams and visions. He knew He needed an increase in the methods to align our plans and thoughts with His plans and thoughts.

It would benefit every person who has put their hope in the modern day materialism, governments, and finances to realize it was Jesus who thanked God that he used the foolish things of this world to confound the wise.

> *At that time Jesus, full of joy through the Holy Spirit, said, I praise you, Father, Lord of heaven and earth, because you have hidden these things from the wise and learned, and revealed them to little children. Yes, Father, for this was your good pleasure.*
>
> Luke 10:21 (NIV)

> *For although they knew God, they neither glorified him as God nor gave thanks to him, but their thinking became futile and their foolish hearts were darkened. Although they claimed to be wise, they became fools.*
>
> Romans 1:21-22 (NIV)

Dreams and visions may seem foolish to some people, but not to the very God who created them, used them, and instructed us that they were meant to keep humanity out of trouble, and eventually prevent people from going to hell. We truly have an awesome God who uses dreams and visions to align people with His plans.

Biblical example — a summary of Acts chapters 10-11:

After Christ died and was resurrected the apostles were on fire and excited about their mission to spread the gospel. Unfortunately, during the initial phase of spreading the gospel, the apostles believed that the gospel and baptism in the Holy Spirit were only for Jewish people. This was not necessarily God's plan, but was the plan interpreted by man's limited understanding. They held this limited understanding until the Apostle Peter had a vision while resting or sleeping on the rooftop of a friend, Simon the tanner. Peter dozes off before the meal was finished being prepared. While in a trance or sleep, he has a vision of a white sheet coming down from heaven with unclean animals on it. God told Peter in the vision to eat the unclean animals, and Peter refused. God scolded Peter in the vision and stated "Don't call what I created unclean, eat it!"

At about the same time (the next day), Peter was trying to understand the meaning of the vision and the command to eat unclean things, when a non-Jewish (Gentile) man named Cornelius also had a vision where an angel told him to send for the Apostle Peter who would bless his family because Cornelius pleased God with his prayers and giving. Up to this point Cornelius and Peter did not know each other or even associate together because the Jews and Gentiles did not associate together. While Peter was wresting with the vision, the Lord said "Go without doubting, there are three men at the door asking for you." The men took Peter to Cornelius' house. Upon getting to Cornelius' house it finally registers with Peter that the unclean animals represented that the Gentiles were now being accepted into God's plan of salvation and the baptism in the Holy Spirit.

The reality that these two men had visions/dreams and followed through on them literally allowed the Gentiles to receive the gospel. Imagine if these two godly men just brushed off the visions they had. These two visions, along with most godly visions and dreams, do in fact change nations and societies.

Don't you think we should take serious our dreams and visions? (The full account is found in Acts chapters 10 and 11.)

This biblical example allows us to see a very important aspect of God's desire for dreams. God has used dreams and visions to form Christian and religious doctrines. For instance, consider the following:

1. The Apostle John's visions and dreams in the book of Revelation are accepted for the most part as defining the end of times and the return of Christ.
2. The dream that Mary's husband Joseph had gave him the understanding and grace that allowed him to wed Mary, and father a son named Jesus who would save the world from their sin; the very beginning of Christianity. (Matthew 1:19-21)
3. Gentiles were accepted into Christianity based on a vision/dream that Peter had. See Acts chapters 10 and 11 describing the vision that changed who was accepted into Christianity.

God states that He speaks to His prophets who He sends to his people in visions and in dreams. See specifically in Numbers 12:6:

Then He said, Listen to my words, when a prophet of the LORD is among you, I reveal myself to him in visions, I speak to him in dreams. But this is not true of my servant Moses; he is faithful in all my house. With him I speak face to face, clearly and not in riddles; he sees the form of the LORD.

Numbers 12:6-8 (NIV)

From this passage it is clear that God has definitely spoken to people through dreams. Some people may say this method of speaking to people in dreams ended after the birth of Christ and after the New Testament has been applied. This can hardly be the case when you consider the following two facts:

1. God spoke continually and used dreams in the New Testament right up into the book of Revelation, which was

estimated to be approximately 70 years after the death of Christ.

2. God spoke through Joel in the Old Testament and Peter in the New Testament and stated, "And in the last days it will be, God says, that I will pour out my Spirit on all people, and your sons and your daughters will prophesy, and your young men will see visions, and your old men will dream dreams." ~ Acts 2:17.

As stated already but worth repeating, is the reality that scientists have proven that dreams allow people to step outside the boundaries of their fears and limitations that they operate under during the day. During our dreams we are more capable of being creative and envisioning things outside the norm. Realizing that God knows more than scientists, it is very probable that God utilizes the fact that He has a greater chance of bringing us up to His level when our minds are not limited by our fears, religious biases, and tradition.

If during dreams and visions our minds are more open to change and the possibility of God's plans, then it stands to reason that we may hear the greatest plans during the night hours. We should all consider what we may be missing! As you will read in chapters two and three, all scriptural dreams and visions could be classified under ... *information and plans that were shared that most normal thinking people would have never believed.* These biblical dreams and visions received were those that changed people's plans and beliefs, yet helped them and society when they were obedient to the dreams and visions. Is it possible God has the greatest chance to use people with elements of change when they step down from their daily thought patterns that normally limit Him, and themselves?

3. God Stated That Dreams Would Increase in the Last Days

In God's Word He stated that in the last days dreams would increase. Most Bible-believing people can take this at face value simply because God said it. Adding to the fact that he stated this would occur are the words found in Matthew 5:18. "Not one dotting of an 'I' or crossing of a 'T' will pass from My Word until all is fulfilled." So, mark it down, people will have more dreams and visions as we approach the end of the Church Age as we know it.

For all the people who struggle with just accepting God at face value, we need to think through why God would increase dreams and visions in the last days. Let me give you what I believe to be the main reason God foreknew thousands of years ago that dreams and visions would increase in the last days.

God knew according to what He wrote in Scripture that the last days in which we live would be extremely challenging for humanity. He knew that the following would occur:

1. That men's hearts would fail them for fear. (Luke 21:26)

2. That all of creation (humanity) would be frustrated and begin to groan, waiting for the manifestations of the sons of God. (Romans 8:17-21)

3. The end days would bring with it perilous time in all aspects of life. (Matthew 24, 25, and II Thessalonians 2)

These known events in our day would create an enormous amount of stress, uncertainty, and confusion. This stress, uncertainty, and confusion cannot be coped with, solved and/or reduced in humanity by mere human understanding, government programs, and church social activity. It can only be minimized, solved, or dealt with by God's supernatural methods. This is why in Romans 8:17-21 God states that all of creation would groan and be waiting for the manifestations of the Sons of God to be revealed. Manifestation means to "make known." God would begin a process leading up to and including His return with the reality of manifesting himself through the sons and daughters of God. This manifestation includes divine intervention, revelation, and the very dreams that God said would increase in all of humanity. God is making known (manifesting) his plans, return, and supernatural guidance through His people. He knew that this manifestation would be critical because, he realized that for centuries people would begin to put their hope, trust, confidence, and loyalty toward themselves, governments, and structures that did not glorify His name.

As we approach the end days with all the perplexities that are increasing, God is ultimately desirous of moving humanity forward toward three things:

1. To glorify His name.

2. To draw people closer to the ultimate conclusion that one day every knee will bow and every tongue will confess that Jesus Christ is Lord to the glory of God.

3. Allow all of humanity to be saved.

When God stated that all of creation would be waiting for the manifestation of the Sons of God, He specifically declared and proclaimed that all of His people would be used to reveal him — not just ministers — no one was excluded. It's time for the Church and ministers to release the sons and daughters of God.

~ Michael L. Mathews

In our modern society, specifically America, we have given glory, credit and put most of our hope and trust in government, America, and social systems, including many man-made religious structures. We even have numerous church/religious structures who insist that God is in the business of saving America versus Americans, Europeans, Australians, etc. Many of these people have put more hope in their America patriotism, government, and legislators than God himself. It is amazing that the majority of our modern day crises including weather, finance, and relationships have revealed that the government cannot solve them. Through these events we should see God echoing out "When will you trust me?" Each day for years most of us are fixated on the television sets waiting to see how the government agencies are going to fix the disasters of our day which include natural disasters, financial crises, and global issues. God is watching and validating where most of our hope and faith has been placed.

Beyond the trust in government, many people have assisted Oprah, Dr. Phil, Montel, Bill O'Reilly, Judge Judy, Rush Limbaugh, and every other talk show host to become extremely wealthy while we become more socially and relationally bankrupt. God has seen where our hope has been put, while at the same time ignoring the very dreams that He 1) used to save people, nations, and societies; 2) said would increase in the last days; and 3) indicated would be part of the manifestations that people would use to set people free. Truly God was foreknowing what our day would become.

4. Personalizing His Message

In God's love for humanity, He is desirous that people respond to Him personally. Many people have learned and believed that you have to respond to God through another person or church setting. This is not the case with God. He is willing to speak to people personally, and he chose visions and dreams to manifest himself. There are too many examples that help validate that when God speaks to people and changes their lives, He does it personally, not necessarily through another person or church. This in no way minimizes the impact we do have on people. In fact a good way to think of the value of speaking God's words to others in a group or church setting is to view it as a means to warm their heart to godly things. This warming is a softening of people's spirit so that they may hear God when He speaks personally to them through the Bible or through a vision/dream.

> *For God does speak— now one way, now another— though man may not perceive it. In a dream, in a vision of the night, when deep sleep falls on men as they slumber in their beds, he may speak in their ears and terrify them with warnings, to turn man from wrongdoing and keep him from pride, to preserve his soul from the pit, his life from perishing by the sword.*
>
> ~ Job 33:14 (NET Bible)

The above passage in the book of Job makes God's dealing with humanity very personal. God chooses to use dreams to allow the potential for no one to perish that all of humanity would be without excuse.

And God chooses to use dreams to allow the potential for no one to perish that all of humanity would be without excuse.

~ Michael L. Mathews

Personal Accountability Rationalized

It is a fact that God is all-knowing and foreknew a time in the history of the world that people would be disheartened and possibly disillusioned by a religious or church life. God's Word indicates that in the last day there would be much deception in the world, religious circles, and the church. In fact this has come to reality as we all know of a great percentage of people who are doubtful of clergy and religious organizations, due to the exposure of many of their behaviors. There is no doubt that both religion and the Church have cast shame, doubt, and embarrassment on their very own methods of survival. However, this reality does not remove the fact that God still desires to speak to people and have them respond to His personal love on a personal basis.

I believe God's love for humanity goes beyond religion or ministers who think everything must past through them. In addition, Jesus Christ Himself decided to take a detour around the man-made church himself. The passage in Hebrews 9:24-25 states exactly that. The reality that Christ could not pass through a sanctuary made with man's hands; should bring great humility, awareness, and godly fear to the modern-day religious structures and the man-made pseudo-church which began to idolize itself, and act as the only passageway to heaven.

Recently God has revealed to me that not only has He chosen dreams and visions to personally help each individual, but that he would increase them due to the perplexity of our time. The church has had ample opportunity and will continue to have opportunity, but the fact remains that He loves humanity so much that He will accelerate and intensify His means to personalize His love.

> *For Christ did not enter a man-made sanctuary that was only a copy of the true one; he entered heaven itself, now to appear for us in God's presence.*
>
> ~ Hebrews 9:24 (NIV)

I have on numerous occasions asked individuals if they have had any dreams. Amazingly enough over 90% admit that they have had dreams. For the few who don't seem to have dreams, they will generally call or e-mail back and state: *"Mike, ever since you mentioned dreams, I started having them."* I do believe that many of them were already having them, but they could not stretch their thoughts or minds to recall them. Once the door is open to start discussing their dreams, people quickly come to the same conclusion that God is trying to help and guide them. Instantaneously, they become very interested in the very meaning of their dream. After discussing what the dreams mean, I leave them with the ultimate question: *"Whose dream was it; mine or yours?"* Upon the obvious answer *"theirs,"* I close with stating, *"What are you going to do about it?"*

I have never experienced so many wonderful occasions where people are required to take ownership of something that was personally give to them. They cannot say that I am pushing religion or God on them. God gave them the dream, and once they realize it may be God trying to help and guide them, they have to wrestle with the dream.

> *The reality that Christ could not pass through a sanctuary made with Hands; should bring great humility, awareness, and godly fear to the modern day religious structures and the man-made pseudo church who began to idolize itself, and act as the only passage way to heaven.*
>
> ~ Michael L. Mathews

In almost every case where I do interpret a person's dream, they state *"That makes perfect sense based on what is happening in my life!"* What a privilege it is to give people the understanding of God's love and direction for them where they have to take ownership. Keep in mind that I am aware of what Job 33:14-18 states, which keeps the dream interpretation focused on God's truth and interest in their ultimate destiny. This is a uniquely different and refreshing manner than the years I spent trying to get people to believe what I believe.

Let me give you an example of how dreams are personalized:

> Last year my mother and father visited our house. My father is a good man, but like many people he openly admits that he has had numerous struggles in life. He has had a tendency to be excited for God and then forget about God. When they arrived at our house on this particular visit, I asked my dad the question "Have you had any dreams lately?" He stated that he does not dream. The next day my dad woke up, and on the way to church he blurted out, *"I had a dream last night in your house."* This was no surprise to my wife Pam and me as almost everyone who stays in our home has the blessing of having dreams. This is not strange because God created dreams, and he created our home to be an environment of His; therefore people will dream in His environment.
>
> My dad proceeded to tell us about the dream, which was: *"I was lying on the operating table having open heart surgery again; however, a very strange thing was happening. The doctors were all around my heart during the operation, but the blood of my body was gushing/shooting out of my legs. The doctors tried but they could not stop the blood loss."* He stated this was the end of the dream. I proceeded to ask if he knew what it meant. He stated no.
>
> Even though I immediately knew the interpretation of his dream, I told him to think about it the rest of the day. That night I asked if he knew what it meant, and he stated that he still did not know. I then proceeded to tell him *"Dad, your dream was a friendly reminder from God that your life was spared through open heart surgery, but you have a tendency to take the blood of Christ and accept him into your heart, but then lose that blood by your actions. God is warning you that you cannot take His blood lightly and then*

you never know when you will not have another chance. God wants you to accept His blood and keep His blood permanently."

I then closed with the words; *"Whose dream was this, yours or mine?"* I have witnessed this same type of dream and interpretation on numerous occasions. The point being; dreams are allowing God to personalize the gospel, as well as the reality that people can and do hear directly from God. My Dad has since become a fan of dreams and just attended a four-day dream symposium we held. He was sure to bring other people to the symposium and even helped assist one man in accepting Christ.

Summary

Throughout this chapter I have attempted to explain why God would choose to use and increase dreams and visions, as well as increase the use of them in the last days. I trust that you have been able to expand your understanding and comprehension that God loves humanity so much that he chose to use a personal method to get their attention. We all need to keep in mind that it was not this author, or the church that stated God would pour Out His Spirit in the last days and people would dream more; it was God himself. This is why it is such a privilege to share on dreams; it was a promise from God and nothing manufactured by any church.

> *And God chose dreams to manifest himself through us, as He knew the man-made efforts of humanity would require divine intervention to allow individuals to see past man's feeble efforts to gain salvation.*
>
> ~ Michael L. Mathews

This may be why the world and wiser people in the Kingdom have realized that during the last 20 years the more music, churches, conferences, studies, dramas, and books that religion has created, the worse the church became. The evidence and statistics indicate that despite all the growth and improvements that man has made, that the sin and accountability within the church has grown in the <u>opposite</u>

direction. Even though this sounds sad, God is now having His way and trying to help man believe that He is the author and finisher of the faith, not the man made efforts we have created. I would back away from this somber conclusion if we could support all the efforts of the modern church with man-made Scripture passages that said something like the following 17 statements which closely reflect what has taken place in the modern church movement:

1. *In the last days I will pour out my Spirit upon all flesh, and I will build mega churches.*
2. *In the last days I will pour out my Spirit upon all flesh, and I will have more songs written.*
3. *In the last days I will pour out my Spirit upon all flesh, and I will have better songs written.*
4. *In the last days I will pour out my Spirit upon all flesh, and I will copy Hollywood and other methods to reach people, because the world can produce better quality than I can. (Ouch, Ouch, Ouch).*
5. *In the last days I will pour out my Spirit upon all flesh, and I will have more conferences for people.*
6. *In the last days I will pour out my Spirit upon all flesh, and I will create more religious opinions.*
7. *In the last days I will pour out my Spirit upon all flesh, and I will create more denominations.*
8. *In the last days I will pour out my Spirit upon all flesh, and I will send out TV evangelists.*
9. *In the last days I will pour out my Spirit upon all flesh, and I will have greater fundraisers.*
10. *In the last days I will pour out my Spirit upon all flesh, and I will help churches celebrate how great they are and celebrate every anniversary with them.*
11. *In the last days I will pour out my Spirit upon all flesh, and I will create greater parachurch ministries.*
12. *In the last days I will pour out my Spirit upon all flesh, and I will use human love to have a love-fest with humanity so eventually they can introduce them to me.*

13. *In the last days I will pour out my Spirit upon all flesh, and I will let the church compromise my position so people do not feel so offended.*
14. *In the last days I will pour out my Spirit upon all flesh, and I will save humanity through a different kind of gospel as my original gospel was too confrontational.*
15. *In the last days I will pour out my Spirit upon all flesh, and I will view politics as more interesting than the gospel and we will focus our energies on elections, debates, and human intellect.*
16. *In the last days I will pour out my Spirit upon all flesh, and I will change the gospel of hell, judgment, and righteousness because I was just joking around about those things to scare people.*
17. *In the last days I will pour out my Spirit upon all flesh, and I will refocus the intent of my son, Jesus, so he will be perceived as "Only Love" as people became too offended in the 21 distinct personalities/responsibilities that I gave Him!!*

I believe that these 17 simple examples when compared to what God's Word really does say, *"In the last days I will pour out my spirit upon all flesh and old men shall dream dreams, and your young men will have visions. And your sons and daughters will prophesy,"* we can conclude that man cannot create methods to personalize the gospel like God can. And God chose dream to personalize His love and direction for humanity. I believe that God chose dreams because He foreknew that in the last days the church would get consumed and twist things enough through some of these 17+ methods that He would have to intervene and go directly to each person through dreams and visions stating things such as:

1. I am real.
2. I am coming back — soon!!
3. I will build a new heaven and new earth and this one will pass way.
4. Every knee will bow and every tongue will confess that Jesus Christ is Lord.

5. Wide is the gate that leads to destruction and narrow is the gate that leads to life everlasting.
6. I want to help you get on the narrow path.
7. I want to save you from hell (Job 33:14).

Almost all the dreams I have had the pleasure of hearing correlate in some fashion to one of these seven simple God-given instructions that we are blessed to be reminded of.

> *"And God chose dreams because He foreknew that in the last days the church would get consumed and twist things enough through human effort that He would have to intervene and go directly to each person through dreams and visions."*
>
> ~ Michael L. Mathews

What an awesome God, who personalizes the gospel to a perplexed world in which religion has become so distorted and hindering. The phrase, "Let my people go," takes on a whole new meaning when ministers and churches realize that God chooses to use all His people in the last days — not just talented musicians, ministers, and puppeteers.

> *"We are so captivated by and entangled in our subjective consciousness that we have forgotten the age-old fact that God speaks chiefly through dreams and visions."*
>
> ~ Carl Jung

> *"The phrase 'Let my people go,' takes on a whole new meaning when ministers and churches realize that God chooses to use all His people in the last days — not just talented musicians, ministers, and puppeteers."*
>
> ~ Michael L. Mathews

Happy Dreaming!!

Chapter Two

Biblical Dreams from the Old Testament

And in the last days it will be, God says, that I will pour out my Spirit on all people, and your sons and your daughters will prophesy, and your young men will see visions, and your old men will dream dreams.

~ Acts 2:17 (NET Bible)

And God chose dreams because He foreknew that in the last days the church would get consumed and twist things enough through human effort that He would have to intervene and go directly to each person through dreams and visions.

~ Michael L. Mathews

Scripture records numerous dreams that God gave to individuals to help guide, direct, and enlighten them. As stated in the introductory chapter, Scripture clearly reveals the following general concepts about dreams:

1. The word *dream* is used over 160 times in Scripture.
2. The word *vision* is used over 95 times in Scripture.
3. God uses dreams to specifically speak to individuals to help them stay focused and eventually stay out of hell (Job 33:14-18).
4. God changed nations and societies through dreams.
5. God stated that He would increase the usage of dreams, visions, and prophecies in the last days (Joel 2:28; Acts 2:17).

This chapter is dedicated to many of the dreams and visions that were given in chronological order within the Old Testament. Not every vision is included, but at least 14 of them are written and explained to give you a wealth of awareness of the power of dreams and visions. I believe after you are through reading all the dreams and their associated purposes and benefits, you will be convinced that we need to pay particular attention to our dreams. I have wondered why dreams and visions have not been more widely accepted, believed and taught in modern Christianity. Upon reflection and realization of the shallowness of our human intellect, I wonder if God protects people from knowing too much too soon (which might cause them to negate all of Christianity?).

It may be plausible to believe that God does not allow humanity to initially comprehend dreams and visions because upon recognizing the amount of revelations, covenants, and doctrines that were born from a dream or vision, many would doubt the notion of Christianity. Upon careful study of Scripture one finds that dreams and visions were the root of many of our Christian and Jewish doctrines. In other words, if an unbeliever in Christianity knew that God spoke to the founding fathers of the faith through dreams and visions, they would think the whole foundation is built around shaky people. Only upon maturity can some people accept that God's ways are different than man's way.

> *"It may be plausible to believe that God does not allow humanity to initially comprehend dreams and visions because upon recognizing the amount of revelations, covenants, and doctrines that were born from a dream or vision, many would doubt the notion of Christianity. Upon careful study of Scripture one finds that dreams and visions were the root of many of our Christian and Jewish doctrines."*
>
> ~ Michael L. Mathews

Dream: <u>A Covenant-Creating Dream</u>
Scripture: Genesis 15:12-18 (Abraham)

> When the sun went down, Abram fell sound asleep, and great terror overwhelmed him. Then the Lord said to Abram, "Know for certain that your descendants will be strangers in a foreign country. They will be enslaved and oppressed for four hundred years. But I will execute judgment on the nation that they will serve. Afterward they will come out with many possessions. But as for you, you will go to your ancestors in peace and be buried at a good old age. In the fourth generation your descendants will return here, for the sin of the Amorites has not yet reached its limit." When the sun had gone down and it was dark, a smoking firepot with a torch passed between the animal parts. That day the Lord made a covenant with Abram: "To your descendants I give this land, from the river of Egypt to the great river, the Euphrates River." (NET Bible)

Overview of the dream: It appears that God was speaking to Abraham about things that Abraham's mind could not comprehend in the natural — thus the dream. The dream included God foretelling to Abraham that he would live a long life and what would happen four generations into the future. In addition, God created a covenant with Abraham and promised that his seed would be great and inherit greatness in the land.

Benefit of the dream: God was making a promise with Abraham and showing him the future. In the dream, God was making a covenant with Abraham, helping Abraham be convinced of the reality of the dream. When God makes a covenant (agreement), no one can break it.

Outcome of the dream: Abraham embraced the dream by following through with the basics of faith (believing God). As history has shown, the seed of Abraham grew just as vast and wide as God promised. In addition, Abraham became known as the Father of Faith, and his descendants inherited the land just as God promised — all within the dream.

Lessons learned:
1) Notice that Abraham fell asleep, and it says great terror overwhelmed him. The end result of the dream was positive, and God had a favorable word for Abraham, but because he was human, he perceived great terror. This is true of many of our dreams — we perceive the terror and forget the message. We as humans are trying to interact with God, and there is a general misperception.
2) God not only reveals information in a dream, but He may also make a promise(s) in a dream. The question is *will we honor the dream?*
3) Dreams may start or seem small or insignificant to a person, but years later the significance is unimaginable. In this case it changed nations.
4) This is one of the many places in Scripture that people do not realize happened in a dream. It is possible that if Christians knew all the revelations, covenants and doctrines that were in essence born in a dream, they might doubt Christianity.
5) Abraham's willingness to listen and obey the dream (i.e. walk it out) allowed him to became the Father of Faith to all generations.

—And God Chose Dreams—

Dream: An Attention-Grabbing Dream

Scripture: Genesis 20:1-18 (Abraham, Sarah, and Abimelech)

"Now Abraham moved on from there into the region of the Negev and lived between Kadesh and Shur. For a while he stayed in Gerar, and there Abraham said of his wife Sarah, "She is my sister." Then Abimelech king of Gerar sent for Sarah and took her. But God came to Abimelech in a dream one night and said to him, "You are as good as dead because of the woman you have taken; she is a married woman." Now Abimelech had not gone near her, so he said, "Lord, will you destroy an innocent nation? Did he not say to me, 'She is my sister,' and didn't she also say, 'He is my brother'? I have done this with a clear conscience and clean hands." Then God said to him in the dream, "Yes, I know you did this with a clear conscience, and so I have kept you from sinning against me. That is why I did not let you touch her. Now return the man's wife, for he is a prophet, and he will pray for you and you will live. But if you do not return her, you may be sure that you and all yours will die."

Early the next morning Abimelech summoned all his officials, and when he told them all that had happened, they were very much afraid. Then Abimelech called Abraham in and said, "What have you done to us? How have I wronged you that you have brought such great guilt upon me and my kingdom? You have done things to me that should not be done." And Abimelech asked Abraham, "What was your reason for doing this?"

Abraham replied, "I said to myself, 'There is surely no fear of God in this place, and they will kill me because of my wife.' Besides, she really is my sister, the daughter of my father though not of my mother; and she became my wife. And when God had me wander from my father's household, I said to her, 'This is how you can show your love to me: Everywhere we go, say of me, "He is my brother."'" Then Abimelech brought sheep and cattle and male and female slaves and gave them to Abraham, and he returned Sarah his wife to him. And Abimelech said, "My land is before you; live wherever you like."

To Sarah he said, "I am giving your brother a thousand shekels of silver. This is to cover the offense against you before all who are with you; you are completely vindicated." Then Abraham prayed to God, and God healed Abimelech, his wife and his slave girls so they could have children again, for the LORD had closed up every womb in Abimelech's household because of Abraham's wife Sarah." (NIV)

Overview of the Dream: It appears that Abraham directly lied to Abimelech and stated that Sarah was his sister. In addition, Sarah agreed to lie as well by stating that Abraham's lie was also true. Once Abimelech took Sarah, God scared the living daylights out of Abimelech through a vivid dream. The dream was, "If you touch Sarah you're a dead man!" This is a frightful kind of dream to know that God gives you a full court press warning — if you touch her you're a dead man. This would indeed give a sobering reality to something you had done.

The dream got the complete attention of Abimelech, and he defended himself that he did nothing wrong. In the dream, God agrees that he did nothing wrong, therefore God kept him from doing something wrong; but God warned him to let her go, unless he would want to die.

Benefit of the dream: The dream has a direct benefit to everyone involved, considering the circumstance. The dream protected Abraham, Sarah, Abimelech and his people. The dream also provided a transition to the very needs that Abraham had. Abraham was going into a foreign land where he had nothing, but he feared that if Sarah was perceived to be his wife, he would lose even what he had — his wife. So through this circumstance and dream God transitions Abraham in a way that probably would or could have never happened in a natural way. Think about it... *What chances do you think there would have been for Abimelech to just hand over all the things to a Hebrew person?* It took the circumstance and the dream to combine to cause the transition. Now tell me dreams are real!!

Outcome of the dream: A person, a marriage, a kingdom, and a nation were all saved and changed.

Lessons learned:
1) God was using a dream to help, protect and provide for people.
2) We need to be careful to not judge what circumstances God brings our way. It is very interesting that in this Scripture passage God did not rebuke or punish Abraham for telling Abimelech that Sarah was his sister. Many Christians assume that Abraham stooped to a very low level of manhood by apparently lying. However, not once did God say that Abraham did anything wrong. In fact, the outcome would imply that Abraham stepped out in faith, knowing God would control the situation. This is exactly what happened. God controlled the situation through a dream. Many of us would have tried to protect the wrong thing — our character, rather than be obedient to God. It should be noted that Abraham appears to have told a half-truth in that he stated Sarah was his stepsister (see verse).

Dream: Jacob's Dream at Bethel

Scripture: Genesis 28:10-22

> *Meanwhile Jacob left Beer Sheba and set out for Haran. He reached a certain place where he decided to camp because the sun had gone down. He took one of the stones and placed it near his head. Then he fell asleep in that place and had a dream. He saw a stairway erected on the earth with its top reaching to the heavens. The angels of God were going up and coming down it and the Lord stood at its top. He said, "I am the Lord, the God of your grandfather Abraham and the God of your father Isaac. I will give you and your descendants the ground you are lying on. Your descendants will be like the dust of the earth, and you will spread*

out to the west, east, north, and south. All the families of the earth will pronounce blessings on one another using your name and that of your descendants. I am with you! I will protect you wherever you go and will bring you back to this land. I will not leave you until I have done what I promised you!" Then Jacob woke up and thought, "Surely the Lord is in this place, but I did not realize it!" He was afraid and said, "What an awesome place this is! This is nothing else than the house of God! This is the gate of heaven!"

Early in the morning Jacob took the stone he had placed near his head and set it up as a sacred stone. Then he poured oil on top of it. He called that place Bethel, although the former name of the town was Luz. Then Jacob made a vow, saying, "If God is with me and protects me on this journey I am taking and gives me food to eat and clothing to wear, and I return safely to my father's home, then the Lord will become my God. Then this stone that I have set up as a sacred stone will be the house of God, and I will surely give you back a tenth of everything you give me." (NET Bible)

Overview of the Dream:

Jacob was in another transition in his life. During the transition he stopped and slept. During this time of sleep the Lord appeared and showed him a stairway to heaven. The angels were coming up and down, and the Lord spoke and stated that Jacob would posses the land and his descendants would expand out from this land in every direction. He also stated he would protect him no matter where he went and bring him back to the land. Jacob called the place "Gate of Heaven" and called the land Bethel during his memorializing of the land.

Benefit of the dream:

1. Jacob received a very vivid validation that the place he was at was truly God's place.
2. Jacob was reassured of his promises from God.
3. Jacob received confirmation of the place where he would come back to eventually.
4. Jacob received a promise for his future descendants.

5. Jacob received God's promise of protection.

Outcome of the dream:

1. Jacob knew he was in direct communication with God.
2. Jacob could relax and know that the search for the "place" he was being called to was found.
3. Jacob had to follow through with what he dreamed. Just having the dream was not enough to honor God. He had to do something, so he built a memorial unto God and the promise.
4. Jacob's family all came to know that this was the land promised to their father Jacob.

Lessons learned:

1) Transitions are great opportunities to hear from God.
2) Dreams should be taken seriously, and in this case Jacob made a memorial based on the dream.
3) When we are uncertain about things in life, God can and does use dreams to direct people.
4) We need to step out in faith after certain dreams and honor God. Jacob stepped out in faith and made a memorial unto God. He was completely obedient.
5) Be careful that you do not shrug off God's dreams. The dream may be your inheritance.

Dream: <u>A Dream that Provided Prosperity and Protection</u>

Scripture: Genesis chapter 31 (Jacob and Laban)

Jacob Flees From Laban

Jacob heard that Laban's sons were saying, "Jacob has taken everything our father owned and has gained all this wealth from what belonged to our father." And Jacob noticed that Laban's attitude toward him was not what it had been.

Then the LORD said to Jacob, "Go back to the land of your fathers and to your relatives, and I will be with you."

So Jacob sent word to Rachel and Leah to come out to the fields where his flocks were. He said to them, "I see that your father's attitude toward me is not what it was before, but the God of my father has been with me. You know that I've worked for your father with all my strength, yet your father has cheated me by changing my wages ten times. However, God has not allowed him to harm me. If he said, 'The speckled ones will be your wages,' then all the flocks gave birth to speckled young; and if he said, 'The streaked ones will be your wages,' then all the flocks bore streaked young. So God has taken away your father's livestock and has given them to me.

"In breeding season I once had a dream in which I looked up and saw that the male goats mating with the flock were streaked, speckled or spotted. The angel of God said to me in the dream, 'Jacob.' I answered, 'Here I am.' And he said, 'Look up and see that all the male goats mating with the flock are streaked, speckled or spotted, for I have seen all that Laban has been doing to you. I am the God of Bethel, where you anointed a pillar and where you made a vow to me. Now leave this land at once and go back to your native land.' "

Then Rachel and Leah replied, "Do we still have any share in the inheritance of our father's estate? Does he not regard us as foreigners? Not only has he sold us, but he has used up what was paid for us. Surely all the wealth that God took away from our father belongs to us and our children. So do whatever God has told you."

Then Jacob put his children and his wives on camels, and he drove all his livestock ahead of him, along with all the goods he had accumulated in Paddan Aram, to go to his father Isaac in the land of Canaan.

When Laban had gone to shear his sheep, Rachel stole her father's household gods. Moreover, Jacob deceived Laban the Aramean by not telling him he was running away. So he fled with all he had, and crossing the River, he headed for the hill country of Gilead.

Laban Pursues Jacob

On the third day Laban was told that Jacob had fled. Taking his relatives with him, he pursued Jacob for seven days and caught up with him in the hill country of Gilead. Then God came to Laban the Aramean in a dream at night and said to him, "Be careful not to say anything to Jacob, either good or bad."

Jacob had pitched his tent in the hill country of Gilead when Laban overtook him, and Laban and his relatives camped there too. Then Laban said to Jacob, "What have you done? You've deceived me, and you've carried off my daughters like captives in war. Why did you run off secretly and deceive me? Why didn't you tell me, so I could send you away with joy and singing to the music of tambourines and harps? You didn't even let me kiss my grandchildren and my daughters good-by. You have done a foolish thing. I have the power to harm you; but last night the God of your father said to me, 'Be careful not to say anything to Jacob, either good or bad.' Now you have gone off because you longed to return to your father's house. But why did you steal my gods?"

Jacob answered Laban, "I was afraid, because I thought you would take your daughters away from me by force. But if you find anyone who has your gods, he shall not live. In the presence of our relatives, see for yourself whether there is anything of yours here with me; and if so, take it." Now Jacob did not know that Rachel had stolen the gods.

So Laban went into Jacob's tent and into Leah's tent and into the tent of the two maidservants, but he found nothing. After he came out of Leah's tent, he entered Rachel's tent. Now Rachel had taken the household gods and put them inside her camel's saddle and was sitting on them. Laban searched through everything in the tent but found nothing.

Rachel said to her father, "Don't be angry, my lord, that I cannot stand up in your presence; I'm having my period." So he searched but could not find the household gods.

Jacob was angry and took Laban to task. "What is my crime?" he asked Laban. "What sin have I committed that you hunt me down? Now that you have searched through all my goods, what have you found that belongs to your household? Put it here in front of your relatives and mine, and let them judge between the two of us.

"I have been with you for twenty years now. Your sheep and goats have not miscarried, nor have I eaten rams from your flocks. I did not bring you animals torn by wild beasts; I bore the loss myself. And you demanded payment from me for whatever was stolen by day or night. This was my situation: The heat consumed me in the daytime and the cold at night, and sleep fled from my eyes. It was like this for the twenty years I was in your household. I worked for you fourteen years for your two daughters and six years for your flocks, and you changed my wages ten times. If the God of my father, the God of Abraham and the Fear of Isaac, had not been with me, you would surely have sent me away empty-handed. But God has seen my hardship and the toil of my hands, and last night he rebuked you."

Laban answered Jacob, "The women are my daughters, the children are my children, and the flocks are my flocks. All you see is mine. Yet what can I do today about these daughters of mine, or about the children they have borne? Come now, let's make a covenant, you and I, and let it serve as a witness between us."

So Jacob took a stone and set it up as a pillar. He said to his relatives, "Gather some stones." So they took stones and piled them in a heap, and they ate there by the heap. Laban called it Jegar Sahadutha, and Jacob called it Galeed.

*Laban said, "This heap is a witness between you and me today."
That is why it was called Galeed. It was also called Mizpah, because
he said, "May the LORD keep watch between you and me when
we are away from each other. If you mistreat my daughters or if you
take any wives besides my daughters, even though no one is with us,
remember that God is a witness between you and me."*

*Laban also said to Jacob, "Here is this heap, and here is this pillar
I have set up between you and me. This heap is a witness, and this
pillar is a witness, that I will not go past this heap to your side to
harm you and that you will not go past this heap and pillar to my
side to harm me. May the God of Abraham and the God of Nahor,
the God of their father, judge between us."*

*So Jacob took an oath in the name of the Fear of his father Isaac. He
offered a sacrifice there in the hill country and invited his relatives
to a meal. After they had eaten, they spent the night there. Early the
next morning Laban kissed his grandchildren and his daughters and
blessed them. Then he left and returned home.* (NIV)

Overview of the Dream: There are two dreams that take place in this scriptural example.

<u>Dream 1</u>: Jacob had a dream from God on how he would prosper Jacob due to the deception of his father-in-law, Laban. In verse 31:10, Jacob shares that the activities of chapter 30 were given to him in a dream. Looking back into chapter 30, God informed Jacob to be creative and help the flocks he watched to start bearing offspring that were spotted, speckled, or striped. These would normally be seen as the weaker flock. Jacob was also informed to make a pact with Laban that all the offspring that were spotted, speckled, or striped would be his wages. Laban agreed to the wage pact with Jacob. Jacob would get all the spotted flock, and Laban would get all the pure color flock. Through time, Jacob's method given in a dream produced a mighty flock for him and few for Laban. In verse 11 of chapter 31 God gives Jacob another dream to get out from Laban with Laban's daughters and Jacob's flock.

Dream 2: Once Laban heard that Jacob had left and ran away, he went after Jacob. He spent seven days tracking him down, and the night before the confrontation (31:24) God appears to Laban in a dream and warns him not to speak good nor bad of Jacob — in other words, be neutral. Laban listened to the dream and did not hurt Jacob and his family.

Benefit of the dreams: The first dream has a direct prospering effect on Jacob. Keep in mind that Jacob had labored for years already without being prosperous. God shares with Jacob a creative way to both breed the flock and make a wage agreement with his unfair boss. By being obedient to the dream, Jacob built his own fortune that outgrew His boss's fortune. All he had to do was listen to the dream.

In the case of Laban, God's dream to him was more of a warning to not harm Jacob. Without this dream, Jacob would have been in for the battle of his life.

Outcome of the dreams: A man who worked diligently was finally rewarded and protected from harm.

Lessons learned:

1) An interesting lesson is the reality that Jacob was able to entice the flock to breed certain color offspring by putting visuals in front of them. This shows the power of watching what we focus on eyes on. It is very apparent that we can literally become the product of what our eyes are focused on. In fact, God knew this and therefore gave him the instructions in the dream. God is very aware that we all will become what we focus our eyes and attention on. The verse that fits this concept is Matthew 6:22: *"The light of the body is the eye; if thy eye be clean your while body will be full of light; but if your eye be evil, your whole body will be full of darkness and oh how great is that darkness."*
2) God used creativity to outwit an unfair boss and bless His servant.

3) God does see fairness and unfairness, but in this case did not just zap the unfair boss or drop a money bag from heaven to His servant. He gave a creative yet practical means for Jacob to be obedient.
4) What happens when people don't listen to dreams? We don't know, but it does make you wonder if many of us miss our direction and blessing by ignoring our dreams.
5) God appears in dreams to both the just and unjust, but offers different messages.

Dream: A Costly Dream that Saves Nations

Scripture: Genesis 37:5-11 (Joseph's Dream)

"Joseph had a dream, and when he told it to his brothers, they hated him all the more. He said to them, "Listen to this dream I had: We were binding sheaves of grain out in the field when suddenly my sheaf rose and stood upright, while your sheaves gathered around mine and bowed down to it." His brothers said to him, "Do you intend to reign over us? Will you actually rule us?" And they hated him all the more because of his dream and what he had said. Then he had another dream, and he told it to his brothers. "Listen," he said, "I had another dream, and this time the sun and moon and eleven stars were bowing down to me." When he told his father as well as his brothers, his father rebuked him and said, "What is this dream you had? Will your mother and I and your brothers actually come and bow down to the ground before you?" His brothers were jealous of him, but his father kept the matter in mind." (NIV)

Overview of the dreams:

Joseph was favored by his father, and now it appears he has found great favor with God. This is evident by God showing him through a dream that his brothers and mother and father would have to bow down before him one day. His brothers despised him, and even His father rebuked him. Many people believe that Joseph would have been wise to not share the dream with His family. I believe he had no choice but to share the dream in order to keep the lineage of Christ alive. You will see below.

Benefit of the dreams:

1. Joseph was receiving confirmation from God that he would be raised up to be used mightily by God; Joseph would save many nations later in life because of this dream and his obedience to share it.
2. Joseph would later save His family and the lineage of Christ by having the dream and sharing the dream.
3. Joseph was able to accept his position later in life because of the dreams.

Outcome of the dreams:

Joseph was hated by his brothers because of the dreams he had concerning his entire family bowing down to him one day. Because of this hatred, Joseph was sold into slavery by his brothers. This hatred and sellout by his brothers allowed Joseph to travel a difficult path that allowed him to meet the king of Egypt (Pharaoh) who would eventually have Joseph manage His entire affairs.

Managing the entire affairs also meant that during a critical famine, Joseph could save his family and continue the line of Christ through one of his brothers who would have died in the famine if it had not been for Joseph being sold into slavery. In other words, Joseph was following God's plan all along, including sharing his dreams with his family when he was younger. Joseph saw the dream fulfilled when His family came and bowed down to Him in Egypt when they needed food to stay alive. Joseph also went on to call one of his sons Ephraim — which means "God has made me to be fruitful in the land of my affliction."

Nations were literally saved because of Joseph's dreams. All of Egypt and surrounding nations made it through the seven years of famine, and Joseph was the dispenser and manager of the very food that saved them during this time.

Lessons learned:

1) As Joseph proved, a dream and the sharing of it may cost you a lot of ridicule and possibly your life. Joseph had to share this dream, contrary to many modern-day spiritual chickens who think he should have been quiet. God honors obedience. I believe this may be the reason that God shared the dream twice with Joseph and his family.
2) God may share dreams more than once to share the importance and significance of the dream.
3) This dream is the only recorded dream by Joseph, proving he was not just a dreamer. However because of his obedience to the dreams, he became an interpreter of dreams. The combination of his dreams and interpretation of dreams was what saved the nations.
4) We must be careful that we understand the meaning of our dreams. In this case no one had to interpret his dreams.
5) Most dreams do not always come to fulfillment right away. It may take years for the dream to become a reality. God uses dreams to help us, encourage us, and direct our paths.
6) Joseph was a spiritual giant who was being trained for a position of authority. He stepped out in his authority early on in life by sharing the deep secrets and prophecy of God through a dream — even though he risked his life and was hated by his own family.
7) We each must wonder how many of us have had dreams that we have hidden because of the nature of the dream. Were we ashamed, afraid, or did we even listen to poor spiritual advice to not share the dream?
8) Serving God is costly but rewarding as you use all the gifts and means in which He communicates to humanity.

Dream: <u>A Dream of Life, and a Dream of Death</u>

Scripture: Genesis 40:1-23 (The Cupbearer and Baker)

Some time later, the cupbearer and the baker of the king of Egypt offended their master, the king of Egypt. Pharaoh was angry with his two officials, the chief cupbearer and the chief baker, and put them in custody in the house of the captain of the guard, in the same prison where Joseph was confined. The captain of the guard assigned them to Joseph, and he attended them. After they had been in custody for some time, each of the two men—the cupbearer and the baker of the king of Egypt, who were being held in prison—had a dream the same night, and each dream had a meaning of its own.

When Joseph came to them the next morning, he saw that they were dejected. So he asked Pharaoh's officials who were in custody with him in his master's house, "Why are your faces so sad today?"

"We both had dreams," they answered, "but there is no one to interpret them." Then Joseph said to them, "Do not interpretations belong to God? Tell me your dreams."

So the chief cupbearer told Joseph his dream. He said to him, "In my dream I saw a vine in front of me, and on the vine were three branches. As soon as it budded, it blossomed, and its clusters ripened into grapes. Pharaoh's cup was in my hand, and I took the grapes, squeezed them into Pharaoh's cup and put the cup in his hand."

"This is what it means," Joseph said to him. "The three branches are three days. Within three days Pharaoh will lift up your head and restore you to your position, and you will put Pharaoh's cup in his hand, just as you used to do when you were his cupbearer. But when all goes well with you, remember me and show me kindness; mention me to Pharaoh and get me out of this prison. For I was forcibly carried off from the land of the Hebrews, and even here I have done nothing to deserve being put in a dungeon."

When the chief baker saw that Joseph had given a favorable interpretation, he said to Joseph, "I too had a dream: On my head were three baskets of bread. In the top basket were all kinds of baked goods for Pharaoh, but the birds were eating them out of the basket on my head." "This is what it means," Joseph said. "The three baskets are three days. Within three days Pharaoh will lift off your head and hang you on a tree. And the birds will eat away your flesh."

Now the third day was Pharaoh's birthday, and he gave a feast for all his officials. He lifted up the heads of the chief cupbearer and the chief baker in the presence of his officials: He restored the chief cupbearer to his position, so that he once again put the cup into Pharaoh's hand, but he hanged the chief baker, just as Joseph had said to them in his interpretation. The chief cupbearer, however, did not remember Joseph; he forgot him. (NIV)

Overview of the dreams:

Joseph had two fellow inmates while in prison. Each had a dream, and when Joseph hears them, he states clearly that "God is the Interpreter of dreams." Based on the fact that Joseph is God's servant, he interprets the dreams. For the cupbearer the dream was one of prison release and placement back into his position before the King. For the baker the dream was release from prison and death within three days after release. Both dreams came to pass. Recognize that Joseph gave credit to God for being the interpreter.

Benefit of the dreams:

1. Joseph was able to show others who would get out of prison that he was able to interpret dreams. This would come in handy at a later time.
2. The cupbearer and baker were able to identify their immediate future.
3. God is given full credit for being the interpreter of dreams.

Outcome of the dreams:

1. The fulfillment of both dreams came true.
2. Years later the cupbearer was able to tell Pharaoh about Joseph's ability to interpret dreams.
3. The cupbearer received his position back — great news.
4. The baker was executed by Pharaoh — bad news.
5. The dreams bridged the way for Joseph to be released from prison.

Lessons learned:

1. God is the interpreter of dreams. He uses His servants to interpret them.
2. Not all dreams are good news.
3. Most people want to know the meaning of their dreams.

Let us learn to dream, gentlemen; then we shall perhaps find the truth.
~ Friedrich Kekule

Dream: <u>Saving Nations — Pharaoh's Dream — Joseph's Interpretation</u>

Scripture: Genesis 41:17-45 (Pharaoh's Dream)

Then Pharaoh said to Joseph, "In my dream I was standing on the bank of the Nile, when out of the river there came up seven cows, fat and sleek, and they grazed among the reeds. After them, seven other cows came up—scrawny and very ugly and lean. I had never seen such ugly cows in all the land of Egypt. The lean, ugly cows ate up the seven fat cows that came up first. But even after they ate them, no one could tell that they had done so; they looked just as ugly as before. Then I woke up.

"In my dreams I also saw seven heads of grain, full and good, growing on a single stalk. After them, seven other heads sprouted— withered and thin and scorched by the east wind. The thin heads of grain swallowed up the seven good heads. I told this to the magicians, but none could explain it to me."

Then Joseph said to Pharaoh, "The dreams of Pharaoh are one and the same. God has revealed to Pharaoh what he is about to do. The seven good cows are seven years, and the seven good heads of grain are seven years; it is one and the same dream. The seven lean, ugly cows that came up afterward are seven years, and so are the seven worthless heads of grain scorched by the east wind: They are seven years of famine.

"It is just as I said to Pharaoh: God has shown Pharaoh what he is about to do. Seven years of great abundance are coming throughout the land of Egypt, but seven years of famine will follow them. Then all the abundance in Egypt will be forgotten, and the famine will ravage the land. The abundance in the land will not be remembered, because the famine that follows it will be so severe. The reason the dream was given to Pharaoh in two forms is that the matter has been firmly decided by God, and God will do it soon.

"And now let Pharaoh look for a discerning and wise man and put him in charge of the land of Egypt. Let Pharaoh appoint commissioners over the land to take a fifth of the harvest of Egypt during the seven years of abundance. They should collect all the food of these good years that are coming and store up the grain under the authority of Pharaoh, to be kept in the cities for food. This food should be held in reserve for the country, to be used during the seven years of famine that will come upon Egypt, so that the country may not be ruined by the famine."

The plan seemed good to Pharaoh and to all his officials. So Pharaoh asked them, "Can we find anyone like this man, one in whom is the spirit of God?"

Then Pharaoh said to Joseph, "Since God has made all this known to you, there is no one so discerning and wise as you. You shall be in charge of my palace, and all my people are to submit to your orders. Only with respect to the throne will I be greater than you."

Joseph in Charge of Egypt

So Pharaoh said to Joseph, "I hereby put you in charge of the whole land of Egypt." Then Pharaoh took his signet ring from his finger and put it on Joseph's finger. He dressed him in robes of fine linen and put a gold chain around his neck. He had him ride in a chariot as his second-in-command, and men shouted before him, "Make way." Thus he put him in charge of the whole land of Egypt.

Then Pharaoh said to Joseph, "I am Pharaoh, but without your word no one will lift hand or foot in all Egypt." Pharaoh gave Joseph the name Zaphenath-Paneah and gave him Asenath daughter of Potiphera, priest of On, to be his wife. And Joseph went throughout the land of Egypt. (NIV)

Overview of the Dreams:

Pharaoh, king of Egypt had two dreams that perplexed him and made him wonder what they meant. He asked around and no one could interpret the dreams. Finally, the cupbearer who had forgotten about Joseph, recalled that Joseph was able to interpret dreams and spoke up. Pharaoh summoned Joseph who quickly interpreted Pharaohs dreams. The interpretation was that the two dreams were one and the same and that Egypt would go through seven years of plenty followed by seven years of famine. Pharaoh realizes the dream for what it is and immediately gave credit to God and recognized Joseph as a man that should be rewarded and trusted with everything within Pharaoh's kingdom.

Benefit of the dream:

1) Joseph was released from prison.
2) A nation was forewarned of a coming disaster.
3) God's favored person was honored with his rightful place; remember the dreams Joseph had approximately 15-20 years earlier.

Outcome of the dreams:

1) Israel would be saved because of Joseph's new position.

2) A nation was saved by being better prepared for the disaster.
3) Joseph would be united with his family who would now have to bow down to him.
4) All of Egypt is exposed/introduced to the favor of God and man of God.

Lessons learned:

1) Joseph's path in life both downward and upward revolved around "dreams." Dreams allowed God's plan for Joseph's life to be revealed and lived out. It is important to note that these dreams were not everyday occurrences, but three to four key dreams and/or interpretations happened over a 15-20 year period.
2) The cupbearer finally spoke up because he was able to recall that Joseph's interpretation of dreams was accurate and came to pass. People will call on you if you are used of God to interpret dreams.
3) Dreams can be tormenting to those who have them. God gives dreams to both believers and unbelievers.
4) Dreams can save nations. Without this dream and without an interpreter, a nation and many others would have perished.
5) People will often seek someone to interpret them. Hopefully they get the godly person. This is a reminder that God's people can and should be interpreting dreams.
6) God's favor was shown toward Joseph through Pharaoh. Pharaoh gave Joseph reigns to the entire kingdom and access to everything.
7) The interpretation of dreams is greatly appreciated by those who cannot understand them.
8) A king who had previously imprisoned Joseph changed his mind and gave God glory. Note in this example that not only does Pharaoh recognize the power of God, but asks the question to everyone: *"Can we find anyone like this man, one in whom is the spirit of God?"*
9) Joseph was being vindicated. The fulfillment of the dream Joseph had as a young man was now taking place. He was

being positioned in a place where everyone including His family would have to bow down to him. Imagine, even his father doubted the first dream, and now we have the king of Egypt helping to fulfill it. Imagine in our present day how many religious people work against God's plans. They doubt the realm of God possibilities because it does not fit what they know, believe, or understand.

Dream: Gideon's Victory Dream — Dreaming the Impossible

Scripture: Judges 7:13-15

> "When Gideon arrived, he heard a man telling another man about a dream he had. The man said, "Look! I had a dream. I saw a stale cake of barley bread rolling into the Midianite camp. It hit a tent so hard it knocked it over and turned it upside down. The tent just collapsed." The other man said, "Without a doubt this symbolizes the sword of Gideon son of Joash, the Israelite. God is handing Midian and all the army over to him." When Gideon heard the report of the dream and its interpretation, he praised God. Then he went back to the Israelite camp and said, "Get up, for the LORD is handing the Midianite army over to you!" (NET Bible)

Overview of the Dream:

In chapter seven of Judges, Gideon is given some directives by God to defeat the Midianites who were of great number. In fact, the number of Midianites were referred to as grasshoppers and their camels innumerable like sand by the sea (v. 12). The problem for Gideon was the way God wanted to defeat the Midianites. He wanted Joshua to take only 300 men and defeat what would probably be tens of thousands. Joshua had 32,000 men capable of fighting, but God scaled it down to 300 men because God wanted the credit, and He wanted to see the obedience of Joshua.

What is interesting was the strange methods God used throughout this example. It can be concluded that God wanted all the glory and to be sure no man could take credit for it. God did not want a man-to-man "who is better" battle, so he had Gideon send the prim and proper or "pretty-boys" back home. The first group who went back home were those that were fearful and afraid. Two-thirds fit the fearful and afraid category, leaving ten thousand. Out of the remaining, he was commanded to choose only the 300 men that improperly lapped up water as a dog … in a not so prim and proper manner. God was looking for the sincere and die-hard men. The reason God was looking for the die-hard men was His plan was to find the men who would do the battle of the Lord without fearing or questioning the method to defeat the Midianites.

God continued his strange method of informing Gideon of the battle through the use of a dream and an interpretation. The dream was given to one of the men and interpreted by another man. What is interesting is the fact that it was the dream that motivated Gideon to know that this was God's plan. The words and plans up to this point were heard and responded to, but the dream was the "trigger" event that was required.

The dream allowed the men to follow through on God's plan which was to go to the multitude of Midianites with 300 trumpets and 300 empty pitchers with lanterns in them (v. 16). When Gideon blew the trumpet there were 300 at one time blowing which caused a sound that would appear like millions of people were attacking. Then Gideon broke the pitchers with the lantern which caused small explosions and fire; at the same time they cried out "The sword of the Lord and Gideon.". This was the interpretation of the dream.

Needless to say, this was a strange battle plan for anyone. God used the events and dream to have the Israelites act out a strange plan. This now explains why God chose the "men" who would stand string and follow orders that allowed Him to gain the victory. Imagine trying to get all the faint-hearted or intellectual men to carry out this plan?

Benefit of the dream:

1. It allowed Gideon and his men to confirm the impossible task they were being asked to complete.

2. The dream served as the "trigger" point for action. Note the excitement of the people.
3. God received great glory.
4. God delivered Gideon and His people in a supernatural way.

Outcome of the dream:

1. Israel was once again delivered.
2. The impossible was accomplished.
3. It illustrates that God expects people to interpret dreams.
4. It illustrates that men of courage are not afraid of God's dreams.
5. Gideon learned to trust in God's supernatural ways.

Lessons learned:

1) Dreams happen and are shared among people of like mind. Notice that the dream was shared and interpreted openly.
2) Dreams that pertain to the things of God are to be interpreted.
3) We cannot minimize the purpose that God chose only the men that lapped up the water like dogs. They were more than likely not the ones too proud. Below is a short illustration called "Where have all the prim and proper people gone?"

I have had a few thoughts cross my mind over the pass few years in regards to God's plans, intentions and concern for poor people, needy people, and the not so "prim and proper" people who do not always fit into our scheme of society or religious circles.

These thoughts have stemmed from the biblical evidence that shows God's care for the downcast, the underdog, the captives, and the poor. In fact we can see places where there is a replacement or exchange of the "prim and proper" with the not so "prim and proper."

Let me start with one of my favorite parables, the **Workers in the Vineyard** found in Matthew chapter 20. The summary is that there were four rounds where the master of the vineyard selected workers to work in his vineyard (early morning, 3rd hour, 6th hour, and 9th hour). More than likely the "prim and proper" were the first selected and then the last were those who were least appealing or least "prim and proper." Do you recall ever being selected last for a sports team or a job, indicating that you were not the "top seed" or most prim and proper person, therefore being overlooked ... left for last?

This experience is somewhat the same as this parable. Nonetheless, the Master chooses to use all people as He cared about the harvest of the vineyard. However, the prim and proper became offended when they found that the not so prim and proper were included in the harvest and even received the same pay. This parable alludes to the possibility that as the harvest of the kingdom draws to the ninth hour of the day, the Master will choose the not so prim and proper to assist in the harvest. However, the prim and proper will need to be careful not to become offended. In fact, Jesus closes this section of Scripture by stating "the first shall be last and the last shall be first" (Matthew 20:16).

Moving back to the Old Testament, we see that God was desirous that Gideon would defeat the Midianites. However, God sent the prim and proper or "pretty-boys" back home who were fearful and afraid. Two thirds fit the fearful and afraid category, leaving ten thousand. The 300 men who were chosen, improperly lapped up water as a dog ... in a not so prim and proper manner. God was looking for the sincere and die-hard men. These were the chosen men who would represent God's miracle, and the "prim and proper" or pretty boys were sent home.

I am wondering and have given thought to the question: *where have all the pretty-boys gone?* Many of them have gone back home, many are hiding in the pew, many are hiding in a ministry or job that allows them to feel occupied. However, God has always and will always look for the men and women who are willing to be more concerned with advancing the Kingdom than those who are worried about being prim and proper, or who are afraid and fearful. Even in Jesus' days on earth the Jewish Scribes and Pharisees looked religiously prim and proper and were the pretty boys of their day; while at the same time right under their nose, Jesus picked the not so prim and proper "rag-a-muffins" to represent Him. The first became last, and the last became first.

Oftentimes when we are looking and worrying about looking prim and proper, this causes us to miss the eternal matters of the Kingdom. I believe that is why Jesus laid it on the line when he said in Matthew 11:12, "And from the days of John the Baptist until now the Kingdom of Heaven suffers violence and the violent take it by force." In addition, back in verse 6 of this same chapter, Jesus says, "And blessed is he who is not offended in me." As I look at the great men and women of God throughout history, it is clear that they were far less concerned with looking and acting prim and proper than they were in advancing the Kingdom at all costs.

If you are a leader in ministry, you may have been searching for the wrong people if you have been looking for those who appear to have all the right stuff, or appeared prim and proper. God may want you to begin another search for the lesser people who can bid the work of the Lord.

If you are a person who always feels like no one wants you on the ministry team, get ready, because God is ready to close out the Church Age and rapture His church. This means that His Word will come to pass, and He will be looking for the last to become first, and the first to be last. This includes using you to assist in the greatest moment in the Kingdom.

If you are a person who is always worried about how you are perceived and ensuring that you look prim and proper, be careful that you do not miss the deeper and more meaningful things of God. The Bible is clear that man looks at the outward and God looks at the inward.

Let me close with the challenge that God informs all of us through Christ's parable of the great banquet (Luke 14:15-24). The parable states that the people who were originally called to the banquet feast suddenly got prim and proper with life, and got too occupied to come. Therefore, the master told the servants to go and get the poor, lame, and the maimed, or the not so prim and proper to attend. The fact was that the prim and proper were replaced with the not so prim and proper. "The last shall become first and the first last."

I am constantly challenged to be reminded that I should not look down upon any person and how God desires to use them. In the name of Jesus, all are qualified. I should also not be more concerned with being perceived as prim and proper by man, more than being obedient to God. Where are all the prim and proper people going to go?

Dream: Solomon's Dream — Hearing a Dream and Answering a Dream within a Dream

Scripture: 1 Kings: 3:5-15

At Gibeon the LORD appeared to Solomon during the night in a dream, and God said, "Ask for whatever you want me to give you." Solomon answered, "You have shown great kindness to your servant, my father David, because he was faithful to you and righteous and upright in heart. You have continued this great kindness to him and have given him a son to sit on his throne this very day. "Now, O LORD my God, you have made your servant king in place of my father David. But I am only a little child and do not know how to carry out my duties. Your servant is here among the people you have chosen, a great people, too numerous to count or number. So give your servant a discerning heart to govern your people and to distinguish between right and wrong. For who is able to govern this great people of yours?" The Lord was pleased that Solomon had asked for this. So God said to him, "Since you have asked for this and not for long life or wealth for yourself, nor have asked for the death of your enemies but for discernment in administering justice, I will do what you have asked. I will give you a wise and discerning heart, so that there will never have been anyone like you, nor will there ever be. Moreover, I will give you what you have not asked for—both riches and honor—so that in your lifetime you will have no equal among kings. And if you walk in my ways and obey my statutes and commands as David your father did, I will give you a long life." Then Solomon awoke—and he realized it had been a dream. (NIV)

Overview of the dream: King Solomon was just beginning his reign as king and he had a dream. In the dream he confesses that he is young and needs understanding and wisdom. Within the dream God is pleased with the request and grants the request to Solomon. Upon the request being honored Solomon wakes up and realizes this all transpired in his dream.

Benefit of the dream:

1. Solomon in essence meets directly with God.
2. Solomon interacts with God and requests a humble request and God responds.
3. Solomon spent less than one night (probably only minutes), and his life was enriched and changed.

Outcome of the dream:

1. Solomon became the wisest man of his day.
2. Solomon also became the wealthiest man of his day.
3. Solomon became an example for generations to come of the wisest man in the world.

Lessons learned:

1) God meets with people in dreams.
2) Sometimes God gives abundantly more than we request.
3) Within a dream or vision a world or life can easily be changed. Solomon's wisdom stretched throughout the land and directed nations and people groups.

Dream: Nebuchadnezzar's Dream — A troubling Dream — Interpreted

Scripture: Daniel chapter 2

Nebuchadnezzar's Dream

In the second year of his reign, Nebuchadnezzar had dreams; his mind was troubled and he could not sleep. So the king summoned the magicians, enchanters, sorcerers and astrologers to tell him what he had dreamed. When they came in and stood before the king, he said to them, "I have had a dream that troubles me and I want to know what it means."

Then the astrologers answered the king in Aramaic,"O king, live forever! Tell your servants the dream, and we will interpret it."

The king replied to the astrologers, "This is what I have firmly decided: If you do not tell me what my dream was and interpret it, I will have you cut into pieces and your houses turned into piles of rubble. But if you tell me the dream and explain it, you will receive from me gifts and rewards and great honor. So tell me the dream and interpret it for me."

Once more they replied, "Let the king tell his servants the dream, and we will interpret it."

Then the king answered, "I am certain that you are trying to gain time, because you realize that this is what I have firmly decided: If you do not tell me the dream, there is just one penalty for you. You

have conspired to tell me misleading and wicked things, hoping the situation will change. So then, tell me the dream, and I will know that you can interpret it for me."

The astrologers answered the king, "There is not a man on earth who can do what the king asks! No king, however great and mighty, has ever asked such a thing of any magician or enchanter or astrologer. What the king asks is too difficult. No one can reveal it to the king except the gods, and they do not live among men."

This made the king so angry and furious that he ordered the execution of all the wise men of Babylon. So the decree was issued to put the wise men to death, and men were sent to look for Daniel and his friends to put them to death.

When Arioch, the commander of the king's guard, had gone out to put to death the wise men of Babylon, Daniel spoke to him with wisdom and tact. He asked the king's officer, "Why did the king issue such a harsh decree?" Arioch then explained the matter to Daniel. At this, Daniel went in to the king and asked for time, so that he might interpret the dream for him.

Then Daniel returned to his house and explained the matter to his friends Hananiah, Mishael and Azariah. He urged them to plead for mercy from the God of heaven concerning this mystery, so that he and his friends might not be executed with the rest of the wise men of Babylon. During the night the mystery was revealed to Daniel in a vision. Then Daniel praised the God of heaven and said:
  "Praise be to the name of God for ever and ever; wisdom and power are his.

>   He changes times and seasons;
> he sets up kings and deposes them.
> He gives wisdom to the wise
> and knowledge to the discerning.
>
>   He reveals deep and hidden things;
> he knows what lies in darkness,

and light dwells with him.

> I thank and praise you, O God of my fathers:
> You have given me wisdom and power,
> you have made known to me what we asked of you,
> you have made known to us the dream of the king."

Daniel Interprets the Dream

Then Daniel went to Arioch, whom the king had appointed to execute the wise men of Babylon, and said to him, "Do not execute the wise men of Babylon. Take me to the king, and I will interpret his dream for him."

Arioch took Daniel to the king at once and said, "I have found a man among the exiles from Judah who can tell the king what his dream means."

The king asked Daniel (also called Belteshazzar), "Are you able to tell me what I saw in my dream and interpret it?"

Daniel replied, "No wise man, enchanter, magician or diviner can explain to the king the mystery he has asked about, but there is a God in heaven who reveals mysteries. He has shown King Nebuchadnezzar what will happen in days to come. Your dream and the visions that passed through your mind as you lay on your bed are these:

"As you were lying there, O king, your mind turned to things to come, and the revealer of mysteries showed you what is going to happen. As for me, this mystery has been revealed to me, not because I have greater wisdom than other living men, but so that you, O king, may know the interpretation and that you may understand what went through your mind.

"You looked, O king, and there before you stood a large statue—an enormous, dazzling statue, awesome in appearance. The head of the statue was made of pure gold, its chest and arms of silver, its belly and thighs of bronze, its legs of iron, its feet partly of iron and partly of baked clay. While you were watching, a rock was cut out, but not by human hands. It struck the statue on its feet of iron and clay and smashed them. Then the iron, the clay, the bronze, the silver and the gold were broken to pieces at the same time and became like chaff on a threshing floor in the summer. The wind swept them away without leaving a trace. But the rock that struck the statue became a huge mountain and filled the whole earth.

"This was the dream, and now we will interpret it to the king. You, O king, are the king of kings. The God of heaven has given you dominion and power and might and glory; in your hands he has placed mankind and the beasts of the field and the birds of the air. Wherever they live, he has made you ruler over them all. You are that head of gold.

"After you, another kingdom will rise, inferior to yours. Next, a third kingdom, one of bronze, will rule over the whole earth. Finally, there will be a fourth kingdom, strong as iron—for iron breaks and smashes everything—and as iron breaks things to pieces, so it will crush and break all the others. Just as you saw that the feet and toes were partly of baked clay and partly of iron, so this will be a divided kingdom; yet it will have some of the strength of iron in it, even as you saw iron mixed with clay. As the toes were partly iron and partly clay, so this kingdom will be partly strong and partly brittle. And just as you saw the iron mixed with baked clay, so the people will be a mixture and will not remain united, any more than iron mixes with clay.

"In the time of those kings, the God of heaven will set up a kingdom that will never be destroyed, nor will it be left to another people. It will crush all those kingdoms and bring them to an end, but it will itself endure forever. This is the meaning of the vision of the rock cut out of a mountain, but not by human hands—a rock that broke the iron, the bronze, the clay, the silver and the gold to pieces.

"The great God has shown the king what will take place in the future. The dream is true and the interpretation is trustworthy."

> *Then King Nebuchadnezzar fell prostrate before Daniel and paid him honor and ordered that an offering and incense be presented to him. The king said to Daniel, "Surely your God is the God of gods and the Lord of kings and a revealer of mysteries, for you were able to reveal this mystery."*
>
> *Then the king placed Daniel in a high position and lavished many gifts on him. He made him ruler over the entire province of Babylon and placed him in charge of all its wise men. Moreover, at Daniel's request the king appointed Shadrach, Meshach and Abednego administrators over the province of Babylon, while Daniel himself remained at the royal court.* (NIV)

Overview of the Dream: King Nebuchadnezzar had a very complex dream that looked into the future of kingdoms rising and falling. The symbolic means in which the dream was received made it hard for the king to understand. As with many dreams, when there are unnatural things as well as beasts they can be quite scary. What we should wonder is why did God give this dream to the king?

I believe that a major reason was to allow God to be glorified and His servant Daniel to be recognized. The reality is that this dream was the very thing that allowed Daniel to exchange the subjection God's people were experiencing during their captivity in Babylon. They were subjected not only to the king, but the astrologers, magicians, and sorcerers. It was clear that King Nebuchadnezzar went to these people before they considered God's answer.

Daniel instantaneously changed this entire environment by allowing God to speak to him in a dream that allowed him to interpret the king's dream. Based on these dreams, given by God, the king made all the magicians, astrologers, and sorcerers subject to Daniel. God had rattled the devil's plan, but it took Daniel's courage to walk out God's dreams. What made this dream different than any other dream in Scripture is that Daniel had to not only interpret the dream but know the dream.

Benefit of the dream:

1. The future of kingdoms rising and falling was foretold.
2. The King worshipped Daniel's God — The King of Kings.
3. God's servants were challenged to step up and be used by God.
4. Daniel's status in the Babylonian kingdom was completely changed.

Outcome of the dream:

1. Daniel and his three companions were forced to seek God for an answer to the dream.
2. Daniel who was at one time beneath or subjected to the astrologers, sorcerers, and magicians, turned things around, and now the astrologers, sorcerers, and magicians were subjected to him.
3. Daniel was placed in a high place of authority.
4. The king stopped listening to his astrologers, sorcerers, and magicians — at least for a season.
5. The king acknowledged the God that Daniel served.

Lessons learned:

1) As stated, Daniel reversed the pecking order in the kingdom from him being subjected to the astrologers, sorcerers, and magicians to them be subjected to him. This came about because of his willingness to believe in dreams, seeking the right interpretation, and having the boldness to share the interpretation.
2) God was able to allow Daniel to dream the same dream per Nebuchadnezzar's request, as well as have the interpretation.
3) God uses dreams with both godly and ungodly people.

4) Some dreams are extremely perplexing and require a person full of God's wisdom to interpret them.

Dream: A Humbling Dream that Turns a King into a Crazed Man

Scripture: Daniel chapter 4

Nebuchadnezzar's Dream of a Tree

King Nebuchadnezzar, To the peoples, nations and men of every language, who live in all the world: May you prosper greatly!

It is my pleasure to tell you about the miraculous signs and wonders that the Most High God has performed for me. How great are his signs, how mighty his wonders! His kingdom is an eternal kingdom; his dominion endures from generation to generation.

I, Nebuchadnezzar, was at home in my palace, contented and prosperous. I had a dream that made me afraid. As I was lying in my bed, the images and visions that passed through my mind terrified me. So I commanded that all the wise men of Babylon be brought before me to interpret the dream for me. When the magicians, enchanters, astrologers [and diviners came, I told them the dream, but they could not interpret it for me. Finally, Daniel came into my presence and I told him the dream. (He is called Belteshazzar, after the name of my god, and the spirit of the holy gods is in him.)

I said, "Belteshazzar, chief of the magicians, I know that the spirit of the holy gods is in you, and no mystery is too difficult for you. Here is my dream; interpret it for me. These are the visions I saw while lying in my bed: I looked, and there before me stood a tree in the middle of the land. Its height was enormous. The tree grew large and strong and its top touched the sky; it was visible to the ends of the earth. Its leaves were beautiful, its fruit abundant, and on it was food for all. Under it the beasts of the field found shelter, and the birds of the air lived in its branches; from it every creature was fed.

"In the visions I saw while lying in my bed, I looked, and there before me was a messenger, [b] a holy one, coming down from heaven. He called in a loud voice: 'Cut down the tree and trim off its branches; strip off its leaves and scatter its fruit. Let the animals flee from under it and the birds from its branches. But let the stump and its roots, bound with iron and bronze, remain in the ground, in the grass of the field. 'Let him be drenched with the dew of heaven, and let him live with the animals among the plants of the earth. Let his mind be changed from that of a man and let him be given the mind of an animal, till seven times pass by for him.

"'The decision is announced by messengers, the holy ones declare the verdict, so that the living may know that the Most High is sovereign over the kingdoms of men and gives them to anyone he wishes and sets over them the lowliest of men.'

"This is the dream that I, King Nebuchadnezzar, had. Now, Belteshazzar, tell me what it means, for none of the wise men in my kingdom can interpret it for me. But you can, because the spirit of the holy gods is in you."

Daniel Interprets the Dream

Then Daniel (also called Belteshazzar) was greatly perplexed for a time, and his thoughts terrified him. So the king said, "Belteshazzar, do not let the dream or its meaning alarm you." Belteshazzar answered, "My lord, if only the dream applied to your enemies and its meaning to your adversaries! The tree you saw, which grew large and strong, with its top touching the sky, visible to the whole earth, with beautiful leaves and abundant fruit, providing food for all, giving shelter to the beasts of the field, and having nesting places in its branches for the birds of the air- you, O king, are that tree! You have become great and strong; your greatness has grown until it reaches the sky, and your dominion extends to distant parts of the earth.

"You, O king, saw a messenger, a holy one, coming down from heaven and saying, 'Cut down the tree and destroy it, but leave the stump, bound with iron and bronze, in the grass of the field, while its roots remain in the ground. Let him be drenched with the dew of heaven; let him live like the wild animals, until seven times pass by for him.'

"This is the interpretation, O king, and this is the decree the Most High has issued against my lord the king: You will be driven away from people and will live with the wild animals; you will eat grass like cattle and be drenched with the dew of heaven. Seven times will pass by for you until you acknowledge that the Most High is sovereign over the kingdoms of men and gives them to anyone he wishes. The command to leave the stump of the tree with its roots means that your kingdom will be restored to you when you acknowledge that Heaven rules. Therefore, O king, be pleased to accept my advice: Renounce your sins by doing what is right, and your wickedness by being kind to the oppressed. It may be that then your prosperity will continue."

The Dream Is Fulfilled

All this happened to King Nebuchadnezzar. Twelve months later, as the king was walking on the roof of the royal palace of Babylon, he said, "Is not this the great Babylon I have built as the royal residence, by my mighty power and for the glory of my majesty?"

The words were still on his lips when a voice came from heaven, "This is what is decreed for you, King Nebuchadnezzar: Your royal authority has been taken from you. You will be driven away from people and will live with the wild animals; you will eat grass like cattle. Seven times will pass by for you until you acknowledge that the Most High is sovereign over the kingdoms of men and gives them to anyone he wishes."

Immediately what had been said about Nebuchadnezzar was fulfilled. He was driven away from people and ate grass like cattle. His body was drenched with the dew of heaven until his hair grew like the feathers of an eagle and his nails like the claws of a bird.

> At the end of that time, I, Nebuchadnezzar, raised my eyes toward heaven, and my sanity was restored. Then I praised the Most High; I honored and glorified him who lives forever. His dominion is an eternal dominion; his kingdom endures from generation to generation.
>
> All the peoples of the earth are regarded as nothing. He does as he pleases with the powers of heaven and the peoples of the earth. No one can hold back his hand or say to him: "What have you done?"
>
> At the same time that my sanity was restored, my honor and splendor were returned to me for the glory of my kingdom. My advisers and nobles sought me out, and I was restored to my throne and became even greater than before. Now I, Nebuchadnezzar, praise and exalt and glorify the King of heaven, because everything he does is right and all his ways are just. And those who walk in pride he is able to humble. (NIV)

Overview of the dream: King Nebuchadnezzar had another troubling dream and again goes to his astrologers, magicians, and sorcerers and tries to get them to interpret the dream. Just as it was in his first dream, none of these servants could interpret the dream. The king calls upon Daniel (called Belteshazzar) to interpret the dream. The dream again had some beasts and strange happenings that perplexed the king. Daniel was astonished for one hour, and the king knew he was afraid or perplexed himself. The king tells Daniel not to worry about the interpretation and give it to him straight.

It is important to note that the dream interpretation was not one of favor or hope. It was a prediction that the king would be removed from the kingdom and made to eat as an oxen in the field for a season of time. This prediction was a result of the king's pride and unwillingness to have mercy. The dream quickly became a reality, and the King was turned into a crazed man and ate as the beasts of the field. This occurred just as the dream portrayed ... for a period of time. At the end of the time King Nebuchadnezzar began to honor God and praise

Him. It was at this time that his reasoning was returned to him as well as his kingdom.

Benefit of the dream:

The benefits of this dream are beyond most human minds. In a sense hundreds of godly and scriptural truths were applied through the dream and its fulfillment. Some of the many include: *Nothing can be hidden from God; Pride goes before a fall; Be ye not deceived, God cannot be mocked, for whatsoever a man sows, that shall he also reap.* The other major benefit of the dream is that God's fulfillment of His purpose for dreams was met. Remember Job 33:14-18 states that God gives dreams to keep people from going to hell. Through this dream and its fulfillment this is exactly what happens.

Outcome of the dream:

The outcome is that a self-righteous and prideful king saw the glory of God once he honored God and not himself. Daniel was also exalted to a continued place of respect due to his obedience to tell the dream as he understood it.

Lessons learned:

1) God is in control of everything, and nothing is impossible for Him.
2) God is in charge of our minds and all that makes us function as rational human beings, and He has the capabilities to remove this reasoning. This destroys the doctrine that God is too loving to ever do an attitude adjustment.
3) When negative dreams do happen, the person of God must still tell the truth.
4) Only God really knows what it takes to bring people to the point of confessing their pride.
5) If you look in Scripture you will find the word *glory* means *honor*. This means where there is no honor there is no glory. You will note that the king gave honor to God after he was removed from the kingdom for a season. When the honor

was given, it says glory followed. Remembering that glory means honor will do your life, family, and ministry great good.

Dream: Daniel's Dream/Vision of Four Beasts(1) — End-Times

Scripture: Daniel chapter 7

Daniel's Dream of Four Beasts

In the first year of Belshazzar king of Babylon, Daniel had a dream, and visions passed through his mind as he was lying on his bed. He wrote down the substance of his dream. Daniel said: "In my vision at night I looked, and there before me were the four winds of heaven churning up the great sea. Four great beasts, each different from the others, came up out of the sea. "The first was like a lion, and it had the wings of an eagle. I watched until its wings were torn off and it was lifted from the ground so that it stood on two feet like a man, and the heart of a man was given to it. "And there before me was a second beast, which looked like a bear. It was raised up on one of its sides, and it had three ribs in its mouth between its teeth. It was told, 'Get up and eat your fill of flesh!'

"After that, I looked, and there before me was another beast, one that looked like a leopard. And on its back it had four wings like those of a bird. This beast had four heads, and it was given authority to rule.

"After that, in my vision at night I looked, and there before me was a fourth beast—terrifying and frightening and very powerful. It had large iron teeth; it crushed and devoured its victims and trampled underfoot whatever was left. It was different from all the former beasts, and it had ten horns. "While I was thinking about the horns, there before me was another horn, a little one, which came up among them; and three of the first horns were uprooted before it. This horn had eyes like the eyes of a man and a mouth that spoke boastfully.

"As I looked, "thrones were set in place, and the Ancient of Days took his seat. His clothing was as white as snow; the hair of his head was white like wool. His throne was flaming with fire, and its wheels were all ablaze.

A river of fire was flowing, coming out from before him. Thousands upon thousands attended him; ten thousand times ten thousand stood before him. The court was seated, and the books were opened.

"Then I continued to watch because of the boastful words the horn was speaking. I kept looking until the beast was slain and its body destroyed and thrown into the blazing fire. (The other beasts had been stripped of their authority, but were allowed to live for a period of time.)

"In my vision at night I looked, and there before me was one like a son of man, coming with the clouds of heaven. He approached the Ancient of Days and was led into his presence. He was given authority, glory and sovereign power; all peoples, nations and men of every language worshiped him. His dominion is an everlasting dominion that will not pass away, and his kingdom is one that will never be destroyed.

The Interpretation of the Dream

"I, Daniel, was troubled in spirit, and the visions that passed through my mind disturbed me. I approached one of those standing there and asked him the true meaning of all this. "So he told me and gave me the interpretation of these things: 'The four great beasts are four kingdoms that will rise from the earth. But the saints of the Most High will receive the kingdom and will possess it forever—yes, for ever and ever.'

"Then I wanted to know the true meaning of the fourth beast, which was different from all the others and most terrifying, with its iron teeth and bronze claws—the beast that crushed and devoured its victims and trampled underfoot whatever was left. I also wanted to know about the ten horns on its head and about the other horn that came up, before which three of them fell—the horn that looked more imposing than the others and that had eyes and a mouth that spoke boastfully. As I watched, this horn was waging war against the saints and defeating them, until the Ancient of Days came and pronounced judgment in favor of the saints of the Most High, and the time came when they possessed the kingdom.

"He gave me this explanation: 'The fourth beast is a fourth kingdom that will appear on earth. It will be different from all the other kingdoms and will devour the whole earth, trampling it down and crushing it. The ten horns are ten kings who will come from this kingdom. After them another king will arise, different from the earlier ones; he will subdue three kings. He will speak against the Most High and oppress his saints and try to change the set times and the laws. The saints will be handed over to him for a time, times and half a time.

"'But the court will sit, and his power will be taken away and completely destroyed forever. Then the sovereignty, power and greatness of the kingdoms under the whole heaven will be handed over to the saints, the people of the Most High. His kingdom will be an everlasting kingdom, and all rulers will worship and obey him.' "This is the end of the matter. I, Daniel, was deeply troubled by my thoughts, and my face turned pale, but I kept the matter to myself." (NIV)

Overview of the dream:

The dream is a mixture of fulfilled prophecies and unfulfilled, or yet to be fulfilled prophecies. Many scholars believe that what is shared in verses 2-7, and 12 are fulfilled and verses 8-11 and 13-14 are yet to be fulfilled.

It is also believed that in Scripture prophecy and visions as is seen in Daniel that the symbols have certain meanings. Many believe that winds represent wars; seas represent people; and beasts represent kingdoms.

Benefit of the dream:

The dream clearly indicates that there will be wars and kingdoms will come and go. This vision clearly shows that one needs to be careful when praying for peace, understanding that the rise and fall of kingdoms is predicted and that God is the author and finisher of kingdoms.

Outcome of the dream(s):

The dream is not fulfilled; therefore the full outcome cannot be determined yet.

Lessons learned:

1) Dreams given to one person can affect entire kingdoms — as in this case, the entire society eventually.
2) God predicts wars between kingdoms.
3) Kingdoms will come and go and yet in the end Christ will prevail.

Dream: Daniel's Vision (2) — of End-Times

Scripture: Daniel chapter 8:

In the third year of King Belshazzar's reign, I, Daniel, had a vision, after the one that had already appeared to me. In my vision I saw myself in the citadel of Susa in the province of Elam; in the vision I was beside the Ulai Canal. I looked up, and there before me was a ram with two horns, standing beside the canal, and the horns were long. One of the horns was longer than the other but grew up later. I watched the ram as he charged toward the west and the north and the south. No animal could stand against him, and none could rescue from his power. He did as he pleased and became great.

As I was thinking about this, suddenly a goat with a prominent horn between his eyes came from the west, crossing the whole earth without touching the ground. He came toward the two-horned ram I had seen standing beside the canal and charged at him in great rage. I saw him attack the ram furiously, striking the ram and shattering his two horns. The ram was powerless to stand against him; the goat knocked him to the ground and trampled on him, and none could rescue the ram from his power. The goat became very great, but at the height of his power his large horn was broken off, and in its place four prominent horns grew up toward the four winds of heaven.

Out of one of them came another horn, which started small but grew in power to the south and to the east and toward the Beautiful Land. It grew until it reached the host of the heavens, and it threw some of the starry host down to the earth and trampled on them. It set itself up to be as great as the Prince of the host; it took away the daily sacrifice from him, and the place of his sanctuary was brought low. Because of rebellion, the host of the saints [a] and the daily sacrifice were given over to it. It prospered in everything it did, and truth was thrown to the ground.

Then I heard a holy one speaking, and another holy one said to him, "How long will it take for the vision to be fulfilled—the vision concerning the daily sacrifice, the rebellion that causes desolation, and the surrender of the sanctuary and of the host that will be trampled underfoot?"

He said to me, "It will take 2,300 evenings and mornings; then the sanctuary will be reconsecrated."

The Interpretation of the Vision

While I, Daniel, was watching the vision and trying to understand it, there before me stood one who looked like a man. And I heard a man's voice from the Ulai calling, "Gabriel, tell this man the meaning of the vision."

As he came near the place where I was standing, I was terrified and fell prostrate. "Son of man," he said to me, "understand that the vision concerns the time of the end."

While he was speaking to me, I was in a deep sleep, with my face to the ground. Then he touched me and raised me to my feet.

He said: "I am going to tell you what will happen later in the time of wrath, because the vision concerns the appointed time of the end. The two-horned ram that you saw represents the kings of Media and Persia. The shaggy goat is the king of Greece, and the large horn between his eyes is the first king. The four horns that replaced the one that was broken off represent four kingdoms that will emerge from his nation but will not have the same power.

"In the latter part of their reign, when rebels have become completely wicked, a stern-faced king, a master of intrigue, will arise. He will become very strong, but not by his own power. He will cause astounding devastation and will succeed in whatever he does. He will destroy the mighty men and the holy people. He will cause deceit to prosper, and he will consider himself superior. When they feel secure, he will destroy many and take his stand against the Prince of princes. Yet he will be destroyed, but not by human power.

"The vision of the evenings and mornings that has been given you is true, but seal up the vision, for it concerns the distant future."

I, Daniel, was exhausted and lay ill for several days. Then I got up and went about the king's business. I was appalled by the vision; it was beyond understanding. (NIV)

Overview of the dream:

This particular vision has to do with the last days of times and occurs two years after the vision in chapter 7. There are four main subjects within the vision: 1) The daily sacrifice would be cut off; 2) The transgression of desolation; 3) The sanctuary to be trodden under foot; and 4) The host to be trodden under foot. Many scholars believe these four topics or subjects are related to what happens and is described in the book of Revelation. There is no doubt that the visions Daniel had and the book of Revelation are related due to the Lord's command to Daniel to seal up these things until the end of time.

Benefit of the dream:

The vision itself helps validate Scripture and the authenticity of what has been recorded in Scripture. The mere fact that this vision and the description in Revelation are so related proves that the visions are yet to be fulfilled, and for validation God had two prophets (Daniel and John) see similar visions thousands of years apart from each other.

Outcome of the dream:

The outcome is yet to be fulfilled (Some believe it has been fulfilled).

Lessons learned:

1) Not all dreams are meant to be interpreted right away. In this case God states that it is to be unveiled at a future time.
2) Some dreams are frightening and cannot be digested easily. Daniel states that after the vision he was ill for several days, and he states it was beyond understanding.

Dream: Daniels Vision (3) — End-Times — 70 Weeks of Years

Scripture: Daniel chapter 9

Daniel's Prayer followed by a Vision
In the first year of Darius son of Ahasuerus (a Mede by descent), who was made ruler over the Babylonian kingdom—in the first year of his reign, I, Daniel, understood from the Scriptures, according to the word of the LORD given to Jeremiah the prophet, that the desolation of Jerusalem would last seventy years. So I turned to the

Lord God and pleaded with him in prayer and petition, in fasting, and in sackcloth and ashes.

I prayed to the LORD my God and confessed: "O Lord, the great and awesome God, who keeps his covenant of love with all who love him and obey his commands, we have sinned and done wrong. We have been wicked and have rebelled; we have turned away from your commands and laws. We have not listened to your servants the prophets, who spoke in your name to our kings, our princes and our fathers, and to all the people of the land.

"Lord, you are righteous, but this day we are covered with shame—the men of Judah and people of Jerusalem and all Israel, both near and far, in all the countries where you have scattered us because of our unfaithfulness to you. O LORD, we and our kings, our princes and our fathers are covered with shame because we have sinned against you. The Lord our God is merciful and forgiving, even though we have rebelled against him; we have not obeyed the LORD our God or kept the laws he gave us through his servants the prophets. All Israel has transgressed your law and turned away, refusing to obey you.

"Therefore the curses and sworn judgments written in the Law of Moses, the servant of God, have been poured out on us, because we have sinned against you. You have fulfilled the words spoken against us and against our rulers by bringing upon us great disaster. Under the whole heaven nothing has ever been done like what has been done to Jerusalem. Just as it is written in the Law of Moses, all this disaster has come upon us, yet we have not sought the favor of the LORD our God by turning from our sins and giving attention to your truth. The LORD did not hesitate to bring the disaster upon us, for the LORD our God is righteous in everything he does; yet we have not obeyed him.

"Now, O Lord our God, who brought your people out of Egypt with a mighty hand and who made for yourself a name that endures to this day, we have sinned, we have done wrong. O Lord, in keeping with all your righteous acts, turn away your anger and

your wrath from Jerusalem, your city, your holy hill. Our sins and the iniquities of our fathers have made Jerusalem and your people an object of scorn to all those around us.

"Now, our God, hear the prayers and petitions of your servant. For your sake, O Lord, look with favor on your desolate sanctuary. Give ear, O God, and hear; open your eyes and see the desolation of the city that bears your Name. We do not make requests of you because we are righteous, but because of your great mercy. O Lord, listen! O Lord, forgive! O Lord, hear and act! For your sake, O my God, do not delay, because your city and your people bear your Name."

The Seventy "Sevens"

While I was speaking and praying, confessing my sin and the sin of my people Israel and making my request to the LORD my God for his holy hill- while I was still in prayer, Gabriel, the man I had seen in the earlier vision, came to me in swift flight about the time of the evening sacrifice. He instructed me and said to me, "Daniel, I have now come to give you insight and understanding. As soon as you began to pray, an answer was given, which I have come to tell you, for you are highly esteemed. Therefore, consider the message and understand the vision:

"Seventy 'sevens' are decreed for your people and your holy city to finish transgression, to put an end to sin, to atone for wickedness, to bring in everlasting righteousness, to seal up vision and prophecy and to anoint the most holy.

"Know and understand this: From the issuing of the decree to restore and rebuild Jerusalem until the Anointed One, the ruler, comes, there will be seven 'sevens,' and sixty-two 'sevens.' It will be rebuilt with streets and a trench, but in times of trouble. After the sixty-two 'sevens,' the Anointed One will be cut off and will have nothing. The people of the ruler who will come will destroy the city and the sanctuary. The end will come like a flood: War will continue until the end, and desolations have been decreed. He will

confirm a covenant with many for one 'seven.' In the middle of the 'seven' he will put an end to sacrifice and offering. And on a wing of the temple he will set up an abomination that causes desolation, until the end that is decreed is poured out on him." (NIV)

Overview of the dream:

This vision or dream was seen approximately a year after the dream shared in chapter eight of Daniel. The vision and dream was sought after as evidence that Daniel was fasting and seeking God. God responded with a futurist vision of what would take place. There is evidence in this passage that the vision and/or prophecy given was for a time out in the future. For this reason, and the interpretation by many scholars this vision is assumed to be for the end of time. Due to the complexity of this vision, we will list more generally the benefits and outcomes. The time required to completely analyze this would take an entire book.

Benefit of the dream:

The dream has indeed challenged all people since it has occurred. Even though some scholars believe the fulfillment of this vision has already happened, most do not believe it has occurred. This vision by itself has created a lot of interesting dialog and topics as to when Christ will return.

Outcome of the dream:

The dream has allowed people to get a general idea on how much time may transpire before the return of Christ. In addition, there have been some signs of the fulfillment of the vision derived by the specifics of the dream. However, we have to keep in mind that even Daniel was perplexed by the dream and its content.

Lessons learned:

1) At times we have to seek after God's vision and/or dream. Most of Daniels dreams, visions, and interpretations were sought after.

2) Not all dreams are fulfilled immediately.
3) Not all dreams can be interpreted immediately. In fact, God may chose to unveil them at a later time.
4) In addition to God's ways not being our ways, his timetable is different than our timetable. In the New Testament God states 1,000 years are as one day to God.

Dream: Daniel's Vision (4) — Israel in the Last Days under the Antichrist

Scripture: Daniel 10

Daniel's Vision of a Man

In the third year of Cyrus king of Persia, a revelation was given to Daniel (who was called Belteshazzar). Its message was true and it concerned a great war. The understanding of the message came to him in a vision.

At that time I, Daniel, mourned for three weeks. I ate no choice food; no meat or wine touched my lips; and I used no lotions at all until the three weeks were over.

On the twenty-fourth day of the first month, as I was standing on the bank of the great river, the Tigris, I looked up and there before me was a man dressed in linen, with a belt of the finest gold around his waist. His body was like chrysolite, his face like lightning, his eyes like flaming torches, his arms and legs like the gleam of burnished bronze, and his voice like the sound of a multitude.

I, Daniel, was the only one who saw the vision; the men with me did not see it, but such terror overwhelmed them that they fled and hid themselves. So I was left alone, gazing at this great vision; I had no strength left, my face turned deathly pale and I was helpless. Then I heard him speaking, and as I listened to him, I fell into a deep sleep, my face to the ground.

A hand touched me and set me trembling on my hands and knees. He said, "Daniel, you who are highly esteemed, consider carefully the words I am about to speak to you, and stand up, for I have now been sent to you." And when he said this to me, I stood up trembling.

Then he continued, "Do not be afraid, Daniel. Since the first day that you set your mind to gain understanding and to humble yourself before your God, your words were heard, and I have come in response to them. But the prince of the Persian kingdom resisted me twenty-one days. Then Michael, one of the chief princes, came to help me, because I was detained there with the king of Persia. Now I have come to explain to you what will happen to your people in the future, for the vision concerns a time yet to come."

While he was saying this to me, I bowed with my face toward the ground and was speechless. Then one who looked like a man touched my lips, and I opened my mouth and began to speak. I said to the one standing before me, "I am overcome with anguish because of the vision, my lord, and I am helpless. How can I, your servant, talk with you, my lord? My strength is gone and I can hardly breathe." Again the one who looked like a man touched me and gave me strength. "Do not be afraid, O man highly esteemed," he said. "Peace! Be strong now; be strong.

When he spoke to me, I was strengthened and said, "Speak, my lord, since you have given me strength." So he said, "Do you know why I have come to you? Soon I will return to fight against the prince of Persia, and when I go, the prince of Greece will come; but first I will tell you what is written in the Book of Truth. (No one supports me against them except Michael, your prince). (NIV)

Overview of the vision:

Daniel again was found seeking the Lord and was fasting for 21 days

On what is assumed to be the 24th day of April, Daniel sees a vision of a man in white with fire in his eyes. No one else saw the man because there was an earthquake as this appearing took place, and they all fled.

The vision in chapter 10 revolves around a visitation from a heavenly being. What and who Daniel saw closely resemble what the apostle John saw in the book of Revelation chapter 1. What should be noted is the awesomeness of the presence of God manifested to Daniel. He could not stand, and he was greatly frightened.

The entire revelation of future events is recorded in Chapter 11.

Benefit of the vision:

The vision itself was remarkable, not just because of the content, but the manifestation of God which was so powerful. Daniel was confirmed as a choice servant of God through the process of this vision. He is also assured that he will receive an understanding of what would happen to his people in the last days, or tribulation.

Outcome of the vision:

Daniel was reassured that his petitions and prayers were heard from the first moment he began seeking God. Daniel received great insight that would only be matched with what was shared with the Apostle John in the book of Revelation.

Lessons learned:

1) The revelation that Daniel was about to receive was spectacular, but you will note the length of time it took for him to hear from God and the wrestling in the heavenlies that took place. This is an indicator that great revelation is not normally just dumped into someone's lap.
2) At times we have to seek after God's vision and/or dream. Most of Daniel's dreams, visions, and interpretations were sought after.
3) The visitation from the Lord was held up in the spiritual realm, which indicates that not all things instantaneously happen.
4) God indicates His pleasure with people. In this case Daniel is called "One greatly beloved."

5) When God manifests Himself people will have the potential to fall down as dead men — or some call it slain in the Spirit. Daniel used many adjectives to describe how he felt when in the presence of God's manifestation.
6) The visitation from the Lord was held up in the spiritual realm, and this indicates there is indeed a war that takes place in heavenly places.
7) Oftentimes when God appears on the scene or speaks to humanity, nature responds. In this case, an earthquake occurred. In the case of Christ speaking "It is finished" an earthquake also appeared.
8) Prayers can be delayed for a season of time.
9) It is possible for a vision to occur among people and only one person sees it due to the circumstances created — just like the earthquake.

In addition to the dreams and visions noted here in Chapter Two, the Old Testament has other visions and that were intentionally not included in detail. Some of the more powerful visions are shared in Jeremiah chapters 24, 25, 38 and Ezekiel chapters 1, 8, 11, 40, 43.

Chapter Three

Biblical Dreams and Visions from the New Testament

"I have also spoken by the prophets, and I have multiplied visions, and used similitudes [dreams], by the ministry of the prophets." ~Hos. 12:10 (KJV)

We grow great by dreams. All big men are dreamers. They see things in the soft haze of a spring day or in the red fire of a long winter's evening. Some of us let these great dreams die, but others nourish and protect them; nurse them through bad days till they bring them to the sunshine and light which comes always to those who sincerely hope that their dreams will come true.

~ Woodrow Wilson

The New Testament is combined with numerous dreams and visions. The dreams and visions recorded are truly significant. They start with dreams on the birth of Christ, and end with the visions and dreams for the future return of Christ in the book of Revelation. The New Testament records phenomenal happenings in the lives of many people that have impacted the history of the world, as well as shaped the beliefs on the greatest events of all time yet to come ... *Come Lord Soon!*

As a warm-up introduction to the dreams and visions in Scripture I want to make mention of the serious belief in the New Testament about dreams and visions. In Second Corinthians chapter 12:1 Paul states something significant about what to boast about, or in other words get excited about. He states *"It is not necessary for me to Glory except in visions and revelations."* He is stating that in himself he cannot glory or take credit; however, he should and does get excited about visions and revelations. There is a clear indicator that the visions and revelations which he received were of tremendous value and helped during His Christian life and ministry. Paul continues on in verses 2-4 that he had a vision, and the vision was so wonderful that it should be unlawful for him to speak about the vision, even if he was able to repeat it. The vision was in Paul's mind beyond description and even beyond a multidimensional all-in-one experience. We know this because in verses 2-3 he has no idea how and where this took place, and he questions (*Was it in the body, or out of the body, I could not tell*). He does realize that the vision was in paradise, and the words were unspeakable.

It is important to note that Paul had received many visions, and the most spectacular was his Damascus road experience (see description of vision below). No doubt Paul had visions on numerous occasions, and thus he states that it is good to boast about the visions because they provided the revelation he needed. Paul also states in Philippians 4:9 that the things we learned, received, and heard in him we should do also so that the peace of God will be with us. Well, guess what? ... What we learned, received, and heard from Paul is that visions are a good thing, and they guided him and will guide us in many situations.

Peter also had visions and knew what most visions felt like; but on one occasion He was like Paul — he was confused if the vision was really in the body or out of the body. Peter just words it differently in Acts 12:6-9. The situation was that Peter was imprisoned and bound in chains in-between two prison guards. An angel of the Lord came and a light shined on Peter, and the shackles fell from him. He followed the angel out of jail, and then Peter states in verse 9: "... *I knew not if it was true what was done by the angel, but I thought it was a vision.*" What Peter is helping us understand is the reality that visions can appear lifelike and real (life can appear like visions, when supernatural things are occurring). It is my belief that what Peter experienced was actually real life, and not a vision. The point is that the two are apparently inseparable at times — so pay close attention when God is at work!!

Happy dreaming and visioning!!

Dream: Joseph's First Dream — Go Ahead and Marry Mary

Scripture: Matthew 1:18-25

> *This is how the birth of Jesus Christ came about: His mother Mary was pledged to be married to Joseph, but before they came together, she was found to be with child through the Holy Spirit. Because Joseph her husband was a righteous man and did not want to expose her to public disgrace, he had in mind to divorce her quietly.*
>
> *But after he had considered this, an angel of the Lord appeared to him in a dream and said, "Joseph son of David, do not be afraid to take Mary home as your wife, because what is conceived in her is from the Holy Spirit. She will give birth to a son, and you are to give him the name Jesus, because he will save his people from their sins."*
>
> *All this took place to fulfill what the Lord had said through the prophet: "The virgin will be with child and will give birth to a son, and they will call him Immanuel" — which means, "God with us."*

> *When Joseph woke up, he did what the angel of the Lord had commanded him and took Mary home as his wife. But he had no union with her until she gave birth to a son. And he gave him the name Jesus.* (NIV)

Overview of the dream:

It is apparent that both Joseph and Mary were respected people and had a good life ahead of them. Suddenly, when Mary becomes pregnant without Joseph having a clue how she got pregnant, he made a decision to not marry her. Imagine the thoughts that went through his mind, on how this could have happened. He was an honorable man from the world's perspective; therefore, he would have done what was right according to the moral law of the land. However, just in the nick of time, a dream is given to Joseph informing him that her pregnancy was induced by the Holy Spirit, and they will have a special child who will be called "God with us" and he will save the people from sin.

Joseph awoke and did not hesitate to do what was right according to God. He also did not delay the decision by talking to all his Bible study friends, family members, or anyone else … he married Mary like he was instructed. This indicates that even though Joseph was an honorable man, his obedience overshadow moral or religious beliefs.

Benefit of the dream:

Mary and Joseph conceived a son who has saved the world. It is important to note that Joseph played a key role in this based on the next three dreams he had. Without Joseph being obedient to the dream, Jesus might have died. Read the next dreams. This whole dream indicates the value that God must place on a father within a family. God did not choose to have his own son raised by a single mother — God saw the value of the family as a whole unit.

Outcome of the dream:

Mary and Joseph had a family in unity, and Mary was not shamed by Joseph. Joseph was learning to listen to the voice of God who would speak at least three more dreams to him.

Lessons learned:

1) When God speaks, we need to listen to what is being said. Imagine if Joseph would have in anyway downplayed his dream.
2) The moral religious traditions and laws are sometimes overlooked in place of the "right thing" or "God thing." Joseph knew what the right moral and/or religious thing to do was; however, he overrode this belief with God's voice. He chose to be obedient to God's voice instead of a belief.
3) God's ways are not our ways or our thoughts. Surely God could have had Mary become pregnant by the Holy Spirit after they were married. However, God knew the pure way and the right way, even if it meant hurting the couple's image within their community.
4) God uses dreams as a chief means to communicate to humanity and instruct people.

Dream: <u>Joseph's Second Dream — A Dream that Spares a Life</u>

Scripture: Matthew 2:1-23
After Jesus was born in Bethlehem in Judea, during the time of King Herod, Magi from the east came to Jerusalem and asked, "Where is the one who has been born king of the Jews? We saw his star in the east and have come to worship him."

When King Herod heard this he was disturbed, and all Jerusalem with him. When he had called together all the people's chief priests and teachers of the law, he asked them where the Christ was to be born. "In Bethlehem in Judea," they replied, "for this is what the prophet has written: " 'But you, Bethlehem, in the land of Judah, are by no means least among the rulers of Judah; for out of you will come a ruler who will be the shepherd of my people Israel.'"

Then Herod called the Magi secretly and found out from them the exact time the star had appeared. He sent them to Bethlehem and said, "Go and make a careful search for the child. As soon as you find him, report to me, so that I too may go and worship him."

After they had heard the king, they went on their way, and the star they had seen in the east went ahead of them until it stopped over the place where the child was. When they saw the star, they were overjoyed. On coming to the house, they saw the child with his mother Mary, and they bowed down and worshiped him. Then they opened their treasures and presented him with gifts of gold and of incense and of myrrh. And having been warned in a dream not to go back to Herod, they returned to their country by another route.

The Escape to Egypt

When they had gone, an angel of the Lord appeared to Joseph in a dream. "Get up," he said, "take the child and his mother and escape to Egypt. Stay there until I tell you, for Herod is going to search for the child to kill him." So he got up, took the child and his mother during the night and left for Egypt, where he stayed until the death of Herod. And so was fulfilled what the Lord had said through the prophet: "Out of Egypt I called my son."

When Herod realized that he had been outwitted by the Magi, he was furious, and he gave orders to kill all the boys in Bethlehem and its vicinity who were two years old and under, in accordance with the time he had learned from the Magi. Then what was said through the prophet Jeremiah was fulfilled: "A voice is heard in Ramah, weeping and great mourning, Rachel weeping for her children and refusing to be comforted, because they are no more."

The Return to Nazareth

After Herod died, an angel of the Lord appeared in a dream to Joseph in Egypt and said, "Get up, take the child and his mother and go to the land of Israel, for those who were trying to take the child's life are dead."

So he got up, took the child and his mother and went to the land of Israel. But when he heard that Archelaus was reigning in Judea in *place of his father Herod, he was afraid to go there. Having been warned in a dream, he withdrew to the district of Galilee, and he went and lived in a town called Nazareth. So was fulfilled what was said through the prophets: "He will be called a Nazarene."*

Overview of the dreams:

In this passage of Scripture there were three dreams that transpired. The first dream was a dream protecting Joseph, Mary and Jesus. It should be noted that Joseph heard the dream and did not hesitate or question the dream. He did not make some decision to fast, pray or seek another person's opinion. He knew the urgency that was portrayed in the dream. He packed his family and left the very same night he had the dream. Joseph and His family headed for Egypt to escape the murders that would take place for all children under two years old. God spared the family and Jesus through a dream.

The second dream was given to Joseph when the time came for them to be safe. The dream allowed Joseph to know that it was safe to return from Egypt with His family.

The third dream occurred after Joseph realized that King Herod's son was in charge of the kingdom and he feared that King Herod's son might try and kill their son, Jesus. Through this third dream he understood that he was supposed to go to Galilee. They went to Galilee and lived in the town called Nazareth.

Benefit of the dreams:

Through these three dreams Joseph was able to spare his son, family, and all Christianity. His obedience to these three dreams is something we should all admire. I wonder how many of us would have followed dreams down to the letter like Joseph. When we read about the great biblical characters many people overlook the incredible faith and obedience that Joseph demonstrated. He was truly a godly man. As a reader you may want to ask, "As a godly man have I heard any dreams for my family's protection, guidance, and future?"

Outcome of the dreams:

Joseph escaped one of the most brutal events in Christianity. King Herod had killed every male two years old and under to make sure no one was a threat to his kingdom. Joseph was also able to bring His family back from Egypt when it was safe to return. In addition, through the third dream he was able to lead his family to Nazareth, which helped fulfill the prophetic words from years before that Jesus would be called a Nazarene.

Lessons learned:

1) God truly leads his people through some of the most trying of times through the simplicity of dreams.
2) God honors obedience — Imagine what would have happened if Joseph did not listen to the dreams?
3) Personal nature of dreams — What do you think would have happened if Joseph would have had the dreams and then went to his Bible study group for an analysis of the dream? What if he would have fasted for 40 days about the dream? What would have happened if he waited till the following Sunday to share the dream with his pastor? I think we all know the answer!
4) Joseph was a true leader who followed what He was instructed to do. True leaders do not always wait for the committee meetings; they act promptly when they know that the decisions need to be prompt.
5) There are times when we must make decisions and make them on our own and reap not only the possible negative consequences but the rewards of making the right decision. Joseph, his family, and all of humanity reaped the benefit from Joseph's prompt decision making.
6) God leads people to protect them. Many times he leads them to another location. Too often people take it too personal when God is leading them on to higher ground. Joseph and his family were led to higher ground. How many of us would have fussed and missed God's protection? I

wonder how much danger I have put my family in by not moving soon enough.

Dream: The Wise Men Get Wiser Through a Dream

Scripture: Matthew 2:3-12

When King Herod heard this he was alarmed, and all Jerusalem with him. After assembling all the chief priests and experts in the law, he asked them where the Christ was to be born. "In Bethlehem of Judea," they said, "for it is written this way by the prophet: 'And you, Bethlehem, in the land of Judah, are in no way least among the rulers of Judah, for out of you will come a ruler who will shepherd my people Israel.'" Then Herod privately summoned the wise men and determined from them when the star had appeared. He sent them to Bethlehem and said, "Go and look carefully for the child. When you find him, inform me so that I can go and worship him as well." After listening to the king they left, and once again the star they saw when it rose led them until it stopped above the place where the child was. When they saw the star they shouted joyfully. As they came into the house and saw the child with Mary his mother, they bowed down and worshiped him. They opened their treasure boxes and gave him gifts of gold, frankincense, and myrrh. After being warned in a dream not to return to Herod, they went back by another route to their own country. (NET Bible)

Overview of the dream:

During the birth of Jesus, King Herod knew about the prophecy that Jesus would come and rule the people. Keep in mind that Jesus was not going to be the type of ruler he should have feared. Nonetheless, he had evil thoughts and wanted the Wise men to come back once they found Jesus and let him know where he was. The wise men had a dream warning them not to return and tell the King.

Benefit of the dream:

God helped the wise man not be responsible for identifying where Jesus was. Imagine the wise men's consciences if they had been the ones to tell the king where to go and murder Jesus.

Outcome of the dream:

The wise man allowed Joseph and Mary to have enough time to escape to Egypt. The unfavorable outcome was Herod went into a rage and decided to kill all children two years and under throughout the land of Bethlehem.

Lessons learned:

1) No matter how wise a person may be, God's simple method of dreams may direct a person's path.
2) No wisdom could have replaced the revelation of the dream.
3) A family was protected through the dream.
4) Christianity was born through the protection of Jesus via this dream.

Dream: Pilate's Wife's Dream – Don't Harm an Innocent Man!

Scripture: Matthew 27:19

> *While Pilate was sitting on the judge's seat, his wife sent him this message: "Don't have anything to do with that innocent man, for I have suffered a great deal today in a dream because of him."* (NIV)

Overview of the dream:

During the trial of Jesus, the Governor Pilate was judging the case. He was listening to the people cry out for the release of a prisoner, Barabbas. Pilate gave the people a choice to either have him release Barabbas or Jesus. Pilate's wife spoke up during this decision making and told her husband she had a dream of Jesus, stating he was an innocent man and that Pilate should not do anything wrong to him. She received this information in a dream.

Benefit of the dream:

This clearly shows that even in the most difficult decision making events, God gives dreams to help make the decisions. The adage "Let me sleep on it," surely applied in this situation.

Outcome of the dream:

Pilate and the public were given a decision to let either Barabbas or Jesus go. They made the wrong choice. They did not heed the dream of Pilate's wife.

Lessons learned:

1) We need to listen to the dreams of people, even if they are not our dreams. God uses people and God uses dreams to help us.

2) Pilate had taken the decision before the people before it was time. By the time he heard the dream and advice of his wife, the crowd's noise overshadowed the advice.

3) God does not miss a beat. He is always communicating, even if it is through dreams.

4) Think of the ironic nature of dreams. Jesus came into the world through dreams and visions, and now the decision to kill him hinged on a dream as well.

Dream: Paul's Conversion Vision — From Saul to Paul

Scripture: Act 9:1-9 (note that Acts 26:19 state this was a vision)

Meanwhile, Saul was still breathing out murderous threats against the Lord's disciples. He went to the high priest and asked him for letters to the synagogues in Damascus, so that if he found any there who belonged to the Way, whether men or women, he might take them as prisoners to Jerusalem. As he neared Damascus on his journey, suddenly a light from heaven flashed around him. He fell to the ground and heard a voice say to him, "Saul, Saul, why do you persecute me?"

"Who are you, Lord?" Saul asked.

"I am Jesus, whom you are persecuting," he replied. "Now get up and go into the city, and you will be told what you must do."

The men traveling with Saul stood there speechless; they heard the sound but did not see anyone. Saul got up from the ground, but when he opened his eyes he could see nothing. So they led him by the hand into Damascus. For three days he was blind, and did not eat or drink anything. (NIV)

Overview of the vision:

Saul, who was called Paul after his conversion, was an extremely religious Pharisee who persecuted and even murdered Christians. He came to an abrupt conversion through a vision on the road to Damascus. In the vision, a light from heaven shone, and he fell to the ground and was asked by Jesus himself saying, "Why do you persecute me?" Saul being frightened asked what he should do. Jesus told him to go into the city, and he will get his orders. Saul gets up but cannot see; he is blinded. Possibly the light/vision was so bright that it blinded him, or Jesus blinded him to get his full, undivided attention.

(God at the same time was instructing Ananias in a vision what would take place when Saul gets there.)

Benefit of the vision:

This vision literally changed many aspects of Christianity. God's choosing this unique approach to shut down some of the persecution by taking one of the most aggressive persecutors and allowing him to be one of the greatest saints who ever lived is just not normal or human, and it baffled the religious world of that day.

Outcome of the vision:

Saul was converted and called Paul. He went on to write the majority of the New Testament and challenged both Christianity and Judaism. Paul defeated many beliefs on who was qualified to be saved, and we can sum this up by simply stating ... everyone is qualified through repentance and acceptance of Christ!

Lessons learned:

1) God indeed is no respecter of people. He calls and chooses who He desires.

2) Visions can be blinding and instantaneously life changing.

3) A vision can take the hardest criminal and turn them into a great saint.

4) A vision can make people do strange things — in this case, fall off a horse and be flat on the ground.

5) God's power/Jesus' voice is overpowering, and no one can or should predict how a person's physical body responds.

6) A vision or portions of a vision may be seen or heard only by the person who is intended to change. Paul was the only one who could hear the voice speaking. This reminds us to not worry what other people hear or see, but be obedient.

7) It is important to note the next vision and how it works seamlessly with this vision.

Dream: Ananias' Vision to Trust God's Decision on Whom God Chooses

Scripture: Acts 9:10-22

In Damascus there was a disciple named Ananias. The Lord called to him in a vision, "Ananias!" "Yes, Lord," he answered.

The Lord told him, "Go to the house of Judas on Straight Street and ask for a man from Tarsus named Saul, for he is praying. In a vision he has seen a man named Ananias come and place his hands on him to restore his sight."

"Lord," Ananias answered, "I have heard many reports about this man and all the harm he has done to your saints in Jerusalem. And he has come here with authority from the chief priests to arrest all who call on your name."

But the Lord said to Ananias, "Go! This man is my chosen instrument to carry my name before the Gentiles and their kings and before the people of Israel. I will show him how much he must suffer for my name."

Then Ananias went to the house and entered it. Placing his hands on Saul, he said, "Brother Saul, the Lord—Jesus, who appeared to you on the road as you were coming here—has sent me so that you may see again and be filled with the Holy Spirit." Immediately, something like scales fell from Saul's eyes, and he could see again. He got up and was baptized, and after taking some food, he regained his strength.

Saul in Damascus and Jerusalem

Saul spent several days with the disciples in Damascus. At once he began to preach in the synagogues that Jesus is the Son of God. All those who heard him were astonished and asked, "Isn't he the man who raised havoc in Jerusalem among those who call on this name? And hasn't he come here to take them as prisoners to the chief priests" Yet Saul grew more and more powerful and baffled the Jews living in Damascus by proving that Jesus is the Christ. (NIV)

Overview of the vision:

Ananias, who was a disciple of Christ in Damascus, had a vision where the Lord spoke to him and told him to go to Judas' house on the street called Straight, and inquire for Saul. God says that Saul is having another vision whole praying that someone will come by the name of Ananias and restore his sight. Ananias, being a concerned disciple, decides to tell God that this is just not a good thing, because he heard how Saul is a bad ... bad ... boy and stands against the Church and even has killed some Christians. God instructs Ananias to go anyway, because Saul is a chosen vessel to carry the name of Jesus before the Gentiles, kings, and children of Israel. God adds the requirement on Saul "I will show him what great things he must suffer for my name's sake." The adage is true ... there are no free lunches. Saul/Paul will pay a great price for what he will agree to. Possibly this is why the degree of the vision and blinding upon Saul. He may have seen more things in his blindness than you or I have seen in our entire life.

Benefit of the vision:

The vision's benefits are beyond putting in words. The first benefit is that through this vision, God helped minimize the persecution by taking the kingpin (Saul) and making him a warrior for Christ instead of against Christ. The vision changed the belief system of many who would have judged who is qualified.

Outcome of the vision:

The connection and obedience of both Saul and Ananias change the leadership within Christianity. The whole perspective of who is accepted, called, and chosen must have shocked quite a few people. A reminder of the cost of being called to be a servant like Paul was given. Even though many had died already, this was a clear indicator that to serve Christ in the capacity people wanted to, it would cost them. How ironic that the very person killing Christians would lead many people to Christ, yet his own suffering would begin.

Lessons learned
1) God challenges us to be open-minded.
2) Visions can be challenging.
3) Visions can be an open dialog between man and God.
4) Visions from God need to be responded to in order to produce the results God intends them o.
5) As you read the last two visions and the next two you can clearly see how severe God was shaking up (reordering) the Kingdom — and it was all happening through visions.

Dream: <u>A Dual Dream that Changes Christianity — Peter and Cornelius</u>

Scripture: Acts 10

Cornelius' Vision — a Call for Peter

> At Caesarea there was a man named Cornelius, a centurion in what was known as the Italian Regiment. He and all his family were devout and God-fearing; he gave generously to those in need and prayed to God regularly. One day at about three in the afternoon he had a vision. He distinctly saw an angel of God, who came to him and said, "Cornelius!" Cornelius stared at him in fear. "What is it, Lord?" he asked. The angel answered, "Your prayers and gifts to the poor have come up as a memorial offering before God. Now send men to Joppa to bring back a man named Simon who is called Peter. He is staying with Simon the tanner, whose house is by the sea." When the angel who spoke to him had gone, Cornelius called two of his servants and a devout soldier who was one of his attendants. He told them everything that had happened and sent them to Joppa.

Peter's Vision — A People Accepted

About noon the following day as they were on their journey and approaching the city, Peter went up on the roof to pray. He became hungry and wanted something to eat, and while the meal was being prepared, he fell into a trance. He saw heaven opened and something like a large sheet being let down to earth by its four corners. It contained all kinds of four-footed animals, as well as reptiles of the earth and birds of the air. Then a voice told him, "Get up, Peter. Kill and eat." "Surely not, Lord!" Peter replied. "I have never eaten anything impure or unclean." The voice spoke to him a second time, "Do not call anything impure that God has made clean." This happened three times, and immediately the sheet was taken back to heaven.

While Peter was wondering about the meaning of the vision, the men sent by Cornelius found out where Simon's house was and stopped at the gate. They called out, asking if Simon who was known as Peter was staying there. While Peter was still thinking about the vision, the Spirit said to him, "Simon, three men are looking for you. So get up and go downstairs. Do not hesitate to go with them, for I have sent them." Peter went down and said to the men, "I'm the one you're looking for. Why have you come?"

The men replied, "We have come from Cornelius the centurion. He is a righteous and God-fearing man, who is respected by all the Jewish people. A holy angel told him to have you come to his house so that he could hear what you have to say." Then Peter invited the men into the house to be his guests.

Peter Fulfills the Vision at Cornelius' House

The next day Peter started out with them, and some of the brothers from Joppa went along. The following day he arrived in Caesarea. Cornelius was expecting them and had called together his relatives and close friends. As Peter entered the house, Cornelius met him and fell at his feet in reverence. But Peter made him get up. "Stand up," he said, "I am only a man myself."

Talking with him, Peter went inside and found a large gathering of people. He said to them: "You are well aware that it is against our law for a Jew to associate with a Gentile or visit him. But God has shown me that I should not call any man impure or unclean. So when I was sent for, I came without raising any objection. May I ask why you sent for me?"

Cornelius answered: "Four days ago I was in my house praying at this hour, at three in the afternoon. Suddenly a man in shining clothes stood before me and said, 'Cornelius, God has heard your prayer and remembered your gifts to the poor. Send to Joppa for Simon who is called Peter. He is a guest in the home of Simon the tanner, who lives by the sea.' So I sent for you immediately, and it was good of you to come. Now we are all here in the presence of God to listen to everything the Lord has commanded you to tell us."

Then Peter began to speak: "I now realize how true it is that God does not show favoritism but accepts men from every nation who fear him and do what is right. You know the message God sent to the people of Israel, telling the good news of peace through Jesus Christ, who is Lord of all. You know what has happened throughout Judea, beginning in Galilee after the baptism that John preached—how God anointed Jesus of Nazareth with the Holy Spirit and power, and how he went around doing good and healing all who were under the power of the devil, because God was with him.

"We are witnesses of everything he did in the country of the Jews and in Jerusalem. They killed him by hanging him on a tree, but God raised him from the dead on the third day and caused him to be seen. He was not seen by all the people, but by witnesses whom God had already chosen—by us who ate and drank with him after he rose from the dead. He commanded us to preach to the people and to testify that he is the one whom God appointed as judge of the living and the dead. All the prophets testify about him that everyone who believes in him receives forgiveness of sins through his name."

While Peter was still speaking these words, the Holy Spirit came on all who heard the message. The circumcised believers who had come with Peter were astonished that the gift of the Holy Spirit had been poured out even on the Gentiles. For they heard them speaking in tongues and praising God.

Then Peter said, "Can anyone keep these people from being baptized with water? They have received the Holy Spirit just as we have." So he ordered that they be baptized in the name of Jesus Christ. Then they asked Peter to stay with them for a few days. (NIV)

Overview of the Vision

The visions that Cornelius and Peter had were both rather strange. Nonetheless, they both responded to the visions accordingly, and history was changed. In Cornelius' dream, God was showing that Gentiles could find favor with men; thus the angel in the vision stated, "You have found favor with the Lord and/or alms have come up as a memorial before the Lord." In this vision he is told to send men for Peter who was about to have his own vision.

In Peter's vision he was being shown a vision of what he would consider an unclean or unquestionable practice: eating unclean things. The Lord replies back with "Don't call what I created unclean." This vision concerned Peter, and thus he doubts it and must question it three times. At the very moment that he is doubting, the men that Cornelius sent are knocking at the door for Peter. Talk about perfect or God's timing being perfect. The walking out of Cornelius' vision ended up confirming and helping Peter walk out his vision.

Peter agreed to go to Cornelius' house, and upon arrival the kingdom of God is instantaneously expanded as Peter recognizes the truth of his vision. He states to Cornelius: *"I now realize how true it is that God does not show favoritism but accepts men from every nation who fear him and do what is right. You know the message God sent to the people of Israel, telling the good news of peace through Jesus Christ, who is Lord of all."*

Benefit of the visions:

The visions by both Cornelius and Peter happened in unison to produce one of the greatest changes in the history of humanity. Prior to these visions Gentiles were not considered to have the opportunity to be saved and baptized in the Holy Spirit.

The whole belief system of Jew and Gentile was changed and allows everyone reading this book the opportunity to be saved for all eternity.

Outcome of the visions:

The dream changes Peter's view of the Kingdom and who is accepted. The dream also educates the entire Gentile population by letting them know about their acceptance into the Kingdom. Needless to say, Christian doctrine was literally changed on the occurrences of these two visions.

Lessons learned:

1) Visions ... like dreams change people, lives, attitudes, beliefs, and doctrines.
2) The obedience to a vision and/or dream is incredibly important. Without either of these two men responding and being obedient, history and Christianity for you and I would be different.
3) God chooses obedient people to speak through. It should be assumed that the reason God chose these two men to see their respective visions is that they each had proven their willingness to be used by God. Remember Cornelius had given many alms to the poor, and his prayers came up before the Lord as a memorial. Peter had already been through his trial and testing period.
4) People struggle with dreams and visions. Notice how Peter struggled with his vision. He questioned, and Scripture states he doubted the vision.

5) Following through on visions and dreams is difficult. What we shared so far is the clean version of how Gentiles were accepted into the Kingdom. Acts chapter 11 shares how Peter had to now go and talk to the leaders in Jerusalem and explain how two visions created a new doctrine. The favor of the Lord must have been present as the leaders gladly accepted the report and the fact that two visions could change doctrine. Can you imagine most modern-day leaders being open to dreams and visions changing the delivery of a sermon, let alone a whole belief system?
6) Our dreams and visions may include other people helping to carry them out. Cornelius included some other people and they did not hesitate. What an amazing thought to know that we all can be used by God though the dreams and visions of other people.

Dream: Paul's Vision — The Macedonian Call

Scripture: Acts 16:6-10

Paul and his companions traveled throughout the region of Phrygia and Galatia, having been kept by the Holy Spirit from preaching the word in the province of Asia. When they came to the border of Mysia, they tried to enter Bithynia, but the Spirit of Jesus would not allow them to. So they passed by Mysia and went down to Troas. During the night Paul had a vision of a man of Macedonia standing and begging him, "Come over to Macedonia and help us." After Paul had seen the vision, we got ready at once to leave for Macedonia, concluding that God had called us to preach the gospel to them. (NIV)

Overview of the vision:

Paul had been on missionary journeys, and up until this point the disciples were forbidden by the Holy Spirit to go into Asia, in which Macedonia was located. Scripture does not say why they were forbidden, just that they were forbidden. Then a vision appeared to Paul where a man was asking Paul to come to Macedonia. Paul did not hesitate to get to Macedonia. It states he immediately went to Macedonia and confirmed that a vision meant the Lord was giving them the green light.

Benefit of the vision:

The vision was Paul's approval by the Holy Spirit to go to Asia/Macedonia. Up until this point the Holy Sprit did not confirm the missionary trip to Asia.

Outcome of the dream(s):

The people in Asia finally had the gospel presented to them.

Lessons learned:

1) God's visions may confirm God's approval.
2) The vision was the approval process, but the question as to why the disciples had been blocked by the Holy Spirit may only be understood when we get to heaven.
3) When we are sensitive to the Spirit, we can know when doors are shut and when doors are open, and that indicator may be through a dream or a vision.
4) A holy man/woman does not hesitate when they know God's approval was just sent through a vision. Paul did not wait and/or determine all the costs to go to Asia — he just went.
5) It can be assumed that Paul was eagerly awaiting the approval of the Lord to go into Asia.

Dream: Paul's Vision — Receiving Courage

Scripture: Acts 18:9-11

> *One night the Lord spoke to Paul in a vision: "Do not be afraid; keep on speaking, do not be silent. For I am with you, and no one is going to attack and harm you, because I have many people in*

this city." So Paul stayed for a year and a half, teaching them the word of God.

Overview of the vision:

Paul was out on a missionary journey and was at the sinful city of Corinth. His vision was given of the Lord to be bold and not hold back. Speculation is that this city was so sinful that Paul would have to be a bold preacher to see results. In the vision, the Lord stated not to worry because no man can stand against you, and God had many people in this city.

Benefit of the vision:

The vision was used to allow Paul to have the courage and stamina required. Paul was able to stay in the city and preach for a 1 ½ years.

Outcome of the vision:

Paul was able to see many people saved as a result of preaching boldly as he was informed in the vision.

Lessons learned:

1) Visions help us see what we need to hear/see in order to do what we are supposed to do.
2) As bold and unashamed as Paul may have been, he needed the vision to stay the course in a sinful area.
3) Paul was reassured in many ways in the vision that he was exactly where God wanted him to be.

Vision: John's Revelation — The Description of Revelation

Revelation chapters 1 and 2 do not specially say that there was a dream or vision. However, it was a revelation or prophecy given about Jesus Christ, the Church, and the future events. Verse 10 states that "John was in the Spirit on the Lord's day when he heard a great voice behind Him." Many scholars believe that this was a vision that allowed the revelation. I also believe that to be the case. However to prevent debate over the entire book, I will not expound on this passage as if it were a vision. Rather, I will use this as means to share a key point that has helped many people lately. It is an excerpt from my book, *What in Heaven and Hell is Happening?*

The intent is to show the great revelation of chapters 1-2 that many people have missed. The information included below gives a reference point for people to use in respect to the rapture of the Church. The reason for the reference point is to help all Christians who want to exclude themselves from any judgment, correction, or instructions by using the rapture of the church as a convenient slide rule. The background question to the reference point is *"What does Christ look like prior to the rapture of the church?"*

The new reference point that I am bringing forward on the timeline is the view of who Jesus functions as slightly before the rapture of the Church. This is the point that Christ is standing in the midst of the churches and is laying out the judgments and ramifications of the church actions. This reference is found in Revelation 1:8-20. The main reason I chose this reference point is the fact that so many people try to escape any view of God until after the rapture of the church. This escapism view allows them to live in that "nice" replay mode and escape all possibilities that we may be judged to some degree prior to the rapture. I believe this reference point is a wake-up call to all people who are serious about their Christian walk.

As stated in a previous chapter, many Christians have become artists at escaping any potential of God being anything but all-gracious and all-loving. Yes, Jesus loves, but He is far more than all-loving — He is all-knowing, all-wise, all-righteous, all-just, and the ongoing and final judge of all human actions. Many people have become escape artists of any connection to the unpleasant side of our Christian faith. They have a preferential rapture doctrine which allows them to slide all negative type Scripture references behind the period of the rapture. The rapture in their mind is the escape route or trap door that removes and excludes them from this side of eternity, where God may be cleaning, cleansing, purifying, correcting, and judging the house of God. Christ serves in this capacity so that He can present a Bride (The Church) before Him without a spot or without a wrinkle (Ephesians 5:25-27).

It is extremely convenient and ironic that so many people choose the escape route considering the reality that no one knows for certain when the rapture will exactly take place. The "all negative things happen after the rapture" belief has increased all the more as our society thrives on convenient and selective doctrine that gives them a positive promise in every circumstance.

Let's take a look at the Scripture that I am using as the reference point.

> "I am the Alpha and the Omega," says the Lord God, "who is, and who was, and who is to come, the Almighty."
>
> I, John, your brother and companion in the suffering and kingdom and patient endurance that are ours in Jesus, was on the island of Patmos because of the word of God and the testimony of Jesus. On the Lord's Day I was in the Spirit, and I heard behind me a loud voice like a trumpet, which said: "Write on a scroll what you see and send it to the seven churches: to Ephesus, Smyrna, Pergamum, Thyatira, Sardis, Philadelphia and Laodicea."
>
> I turned around to see the voice that was speaking to me. And when I turned I saw seven golden lampstands, and among the lampstands was someone "like a son of man," dressed in a robe reaching down to his feet and with a golden sash around his chest. His head and hair were white like wool, as white as snow, and his eyes were like blazing fire. His feet were like bronze glowing in a furnace, and his voice was like the sound of rushing waters. In his right hand he held seven stars, and out of his mouth came a sharp double-edged sword. His face was like the sun shining in all its brilliance.
>
> When I saw him, I fell at his feet as though dead. Then he placed his right hand on me and said: "Do not be afraid. I am the First and the Last. I am the Living One; I was dead, and behold I am alive for ever and ever! And I hold the keys of death and Hades.

"Write, therefore, what you have seen, what is now and what will take place later. The mystery of the seven stars that you saw in my right hand and of the seven golden lampstands is this: The seven stars are the angels of the seven churches, and the seven lampstands are the seven churches. (Revelation 1:8-20 NIV)

This particular Scripture passage is a wonderful description of Christ, His position, and relation to the churches and pastors prior to the rapture of the Church. This view is critical for us as we can see exactly what is happening before the rapture of the Church. Many theologians and Bible scholars have concluded that because there is no mention of the Church after Revelation chapter 3 that the Church has been raptured. Please note this is not a proven fact, but speculation based on two critical biblical observations:

1. There is no mention of the churches after chapter 3 of Revelation.
2. Jesus spoke to John in Revelation 1:19 stating that he is to record three things
    A) The things he just saw (referring to chapter 1).
    B) The things which are (referring to chapters 2-3).
    C) The things that are to happen hereafter (referring to things in chapter 4:1 through chapter 21:5).

I will not focus time trying to prove or disprove this stance by theologians and Bible scholars as I honestly don't have all the evidence, and Jesus said it was not for us to know the exact time. I will however make note of three personal observations which should be considered:

1. The word "church" is used one more time in the last chapter of Revelation. Revelation 22:16 states, "I, Jesus, have sent my angel to give you this testimony for the churches. I am the root and the offspring of David, and the Bright and Morning Star."
2. If I were to write a letter to my wife and two daughters knowing I would not see them for a long time, I would start the letter by encouraging my wife. I would tell her to

stay focused on raising the children and other instructions. After I was done writing her portion, I would switch the writing to convey personal and instructive information to each of my daughters. Lastly, I would close the letter with summary information. I would not want anyone to assume because I did not mention my wife again during the portions of the letter where I am referring to my daughters that she has suddenly disappeared or is gone from the scene. It should be interpreted that it was just the flow of my letter.

3. In the closing of my letter I would make a statement that made a clear statement that I love them and include all who were addressed and assumed alive. The closing statement of my letter would be much like *"Pam, Jessica, and Tiffany, please listen to the words I stated and know that I love you and I will be coming back."* In much the same manner, God closes the last chapter of the book of Revelation by stating *"I, Jesus, have sent my angel to give you this testimony for the churches. I am the Root and the Offspring of David, and the Bright and Morning Star"* (Revelation 22:16).

What these points may portray is that it is may be presumptuous to conclude that the church is removed after chapter 3. Keep in mind that these are my observations which of course are common sense thoughts and should not be used to define doctrine or agree or disagree with Bible scholars and theologians who have spent lifetimes studying the subject.

What is of most importance to us in the context of this book is to draw the closest and clearest reference point to where we are today, based on Scripture. It is an attempt to alert people that we were given a clear view of what Christ appears as just prior to the rapture. However, this view may shake people up because it does exactly what Scripture is intended to do: "judge the thoughts and intentions of the heart."

> *For the word of God is living and active. Sharper than any double-edged sword, it penetrates even to dividing soul and spirit, joints and marrow; it judges the thoughts and attitudes of the heart.*
>
> ~ (Hebrews 4:12 NIV)

My main purpose is to awaken people who are always skating around the truth, are too afraid to admit the truth, want to believe the Church is above reproach, we are all going to heaven, and/or we will all escape through the rapture door prior to any negative circumstances occurring to any of the church folks. My hope is also that many people will start to wonder why we choose to stay in replay mode and only see Christ as the baby in the manger or the all-loving Savior on the cross. We must mature to a point we can admit and live for the whole truth, not selective truth, tradition, or "group think" behavior that keeps the guests coming to our churches, small groups, or conferences.

A Closer Look at the Reference Point

With Revelation chapters 1, 2, and 3 dealing specifically with the Church we must conclude that the Church is at the center of attention and the revelation to the Apostle John is for the Church. As we review the Scripture in chapter 1, there are numerous building blocks of church theology that should be noted. I would like to take this opportunity to describe some of the basic building blocks. The basics may hurt a little bit, but hopefully they will get your attention.

Building Blocks:

1. The Apostle John loves Jesus Christ, and believes in the Church. This is one of the main reasons that Christ gives him this revelation.
2. Even though the Apostle John believes in the Church He is all by himself on the Isle of Patmos. It is evident that there is no church building, pastor, or denomination on the Isle of Patmos. He is isolated by himself. Without the outcome of the revelation he received, many of us would have passed judgment upon him and said he left the church. Keep in

mind that many of us have the narrow view that the church can only be existent if there is a building, pastor, and/or congregation. The church building as we know it is only a figure of the truth and not the full truth. Yes, according to Scripture the church is only a figure of the truth. Sit back and meditate and pray on the specific Scripture below, and come to your own conclusion. Unfortunately, we have oftentimes made the church buildings what we worship and put our hope in.

For Christ did not enter a man-made sanctuary that was only a copy of the true one; he entered heaven itself, now to appear for us in God's presence. ~ Hebrews 9:24 (NIV) and

For Christ is not entered into the holy places made with hands, which are the figures of the true; but into heaven itself, now to appear in the presence of God for us. ~ Hebrews 9:24 (KJV)

It is amazing that the greatest moments in Christian history were not in a church building or congregation … but most often a place of isolation where individuals have tested their faith and have looked solely upon God. Examples of this include Jesus on the cross; Stephen being stoned in public by himself; Paul in prison by himself; John on the Isle of Patmos by himself. Looking back further, we also see in the Old Testament the place of change happened often without groups of people. Examples of this include Moses on the mountain by himself; Moses in the cleft of the rock by himself; Jacob by himself in Bethel wrestling with the angel; David face to face with Goliath by himself, a lion by himself, a bear by himself; Jonah in the whale by himself; Job alone by himself with only judgmental friends; David walking through the valley of the shadow of death by himself. All this to say we need to be careful that we are not so "people and congregational" minded that anyone outside of a congregation is doomed and pegged as having left the church and damned for life. Some of your greatest days may be outside the four walls of the church building when you are forced to be by yourself, with God. We need to be careful that we do not overplay the concept that we need each other so much that we are never forced to seek God face-to-face by ourselves.

3. John was in the Spirit on the Lord's day (Revelation 1:10-11). Notice that John was in the Spirit without a church building, without a choir and without any corporate worship. John was without a church, yet had the belief that true worship was between him and God. He somehow knew that no man or church can work him into worship, or out of worship; he simply knew God was <u>Wor</u>thy of His friend<u>ship</u> (Worship). For every person who cannot enter into times of worship without all the warm-ups, choirs, talents, and people … please pray for understanding of true worship. I say all this with much conviction because in Revelation 1:17-19 John falls down as a dead man in the presence of Jesus who says he wants him to record some of the greatest words in the history of the world. John did not put the Lord on hold and say, "I can't enter into worship without hymns or praise songs." God was there because John worshipped in truth and spirit. The modern church has trained and convinced people that they cannot worship until they have the right tunes of music, and have gone through the motions of "patterned behavior" which we have titled modern worship. In many cases we have trained the musical ear to only think that we can hear from God when the music and people are all in tune, and we have a sweet sound. The reality is that being in tune and making sweet music does not indicate true worship. I agree it may feel like worship because all the talent has created a sense of group karaoke, giving us just the right feeling of emotion and satisfaction.
4. John fell down as a dead man in God's presence. He literally responded to God in whole scale "awe" before a sermon was ever preached. It is scripturally factual that when people come into the presence of God they cannot stand because of the powerful glory of God.
Imagine a church that could claim that they have the presence of God because they worship on the Lord's Day in

truth and spirit. A place where people fall prior to the man-made worship, songs, and sermons ever begin. The mere presence of God would cleanse the people we have been trying to cleanse for years. It is possible that God moved so mightily upon John that He had to have him in isolation so that he was neither distracted by man's worship, nor that a person or denomination could try and take the credit. Imagine God revealing this revelation to John in front of a church or denomination — they might have taken credit and immediately started selling books, CDs, and T-shirts that followed the awesome Revelation; and claim their church or denomination as having the "sole" truth, or "sole" blessing. Scripture states that God will not share His glory with any man. Therefore, the more of humanity that is present (showcasing) the less of God that is present. The opposite is also true; the more of God we allow to be present, the less of humanity that is needed. This is probably why John could be all by himself and have one of the most wonderful Sunday services known to the history of the world. Another thought is ... God knew that if John was near people and churches, John might have been frightened to share such a message in fear it would have caused an uproar among his network of minister friends and ministries, which in turn would cut off his support mechanism.

5. The description of what John sees that is so overwhelming is the way Christ looks. The look is described in verses 12-18 of Revelation chapter 1.
   a. Christ is in the midst of seven golden candlesticks/lampstands (verse 12-13). The candlesticks or lampstands represented the churches (verse 20).
   b. He is clothed in a garment down to His feet and with a golden sash around His chest. (verse 13).
   c. His head and hair were like wool; white as snow. (verse 14).
   d. His eyes were as a flame of fire (verse 14).
   e. His feet were like fine brass as if burned in a furnace (verse 15).

    f.   His voice sounded like many waters (verse 15).
    g. He had seven stars in His right hand (verse 16). The seven stars represent the angels; also interpreted as ministers (verse 20).
    h. He had a sharp two-edged sword in His mouth (verse 16).
    i.   His countenance was like the Sun in strength (verse 16).
6. Jesus shares a mystery with John who then shares it for the world to hear. The mystery is found in chapter 1 verse 20 which states: *"The mystery of the seven stars which thou sawest in my right hand, and the seven golden candlesticks. The seven stars are the angels of the seven churches: and the seven candlesticks which thou sawest are the seven churches."*

With this Scripture we have finally reached the climax of this book — which is intended to get the attention of people who have lived their lives in the past and/or the future. Let me start this climactic moment by asking a few critical questions.

1. Have you ever been to a Christian drama or movie representation where Christ was portrayed as what we just stated above, prior to the rapture of the Church? A summary of that representation would be a picture of Christ standing in the midst of churches with a two-edged sword in His mouth, fire in His eyes, a robe of righteousness, holding ministers in His right hand? If you are like most of us, you have never seen a drama like this. Why not?
2. When was the last time you went to a Christmas or Easter drama that portrayed Christ as if He is still a baby in the manger, or on the Cross, or ascending to heaven? If you are like most of us, you have gone to numerous dramas like this.

The importance of these two questions is that when we as Christians choose to always share that Christ and/or the gospel are quaint and non-confrontational, we have missed the gospel and the full testimony of Jesus Christ. How do I know this? Simply put: in Revelation 1:9, John states his whole mission is for the testimony of Jesus Christ.

> *I John, who also am your brother, and companion in tribulation, and in the kingdom and patience of Jesus Christ, was in the isle that is called Patmos, for the word of God, and for the testimony of Jesus Christ.*
>
> ~ Revelation 1:9 (KJV)

It is clear that John's mission is to share the testimony of Jesus which is clearly beyond two to three major events repeated every year. If I was to have someone share the testimony of my life, I would be disappointed as well as misrepresented if the writer only focused on my salvation and the first few years of my Christianity. I would desire they focus on my entire life, my time line, the different roles I played, and the recent victories that showed that I was far more of an individual than just the first few years of my life.

The same concept should be applied here as well. John, a dedicated disciple, was chosen to represent the fullness of the Kingdom and Jesus Christ; which is well beyond a replay of the same events everyone had already heard. Jesus was desirous to get the full message to all the churches that existed in that day. Jesus did not tell John to send the Christmas or Easter Story in a manuscript so they could relive what had already taken place. He was desirous to give them a truthful and serious message in Revelation chapters 1-3.

In fact, to persuade the readers of Revelation 2-3, Jesus has John address each of the seven churches with a different (role) or name for Himself. Look closely at the names Jesus is introduced as in each of the introductions.

1. To the angel of the church of Ephesus write, "These things says He who holds the seven stars in His right hand, who walks in the midst of the seven golden candlesticks:" Revelation 2:1 (NKJ)

2. And to the angel of the church in Smyrna write, "These things says the First and Last, who was dead and came to life." Revelation 2:8 (NKJ)
3. And to the angel of the church in Pergamos write, "These things says He who has the sharp two-edged sword." Revelation 2:12 (NKJ)
4. And to the angel of the church in Thyatira write, "These things says the Son of God, who has eyes like a flame of fire, and His feet like fine brass." Revelation 2:18 (NKJ)
5. And to the angel of the church in Sardis write, "These things says He who has the seven Spirits of God and the seven stars." Revelation 3:1 (NKJ)
6. And to the angel of the church in Philadelphia write, "These things says He who is holy, 'He who is true, He who has the key of David, He who opens and no one shuts, and shuts and no one opens.'" Revelation 3:7 (NKJ)
7. And to the angel of the church of the Laodiceans write, "These things says the Amen, The Faithful and True Witness, the Beginning of the creation of God." Revelation 3:14 (NKJ)

The serious nature of the message to each of the churches was that Jesus' role was as Lord, counselor, and judge of the churches and people. Anyone with a 6th grade education (unless deceived by the enemy, or having selfish motives) can read chapters 1-3 and determine that Jesus is in the midst of the churches and warns them of the need to stay focused, repent, and be serious about their love for Him, or their light will be removed. The fact that it is this simple really helps explain the reality that Jesus is judging the motives of the church and ministers of the churches. Generally speaking, a judge warns of the ultimate rewards and punishments of doing either the right or the wrong thing. In every case, Jesus makes clear statements warning us of the dangers of not staying focused on the testimony of Christ. He also tells everyone to have an "ear to hear what the Spirit is saying to the churches."

It is critical to note that in chapters 2-3, Jesus states churches as plural, when stating "He that hath an ear let him hear what the spirit is saying to the Churches." Even though the message is for a specific geographical area church (i.e. city of Ephesus), the reality is that the message went to the churches that existed in that area. What if there would have been ten additional geographical area churches because the world and church were developed beyond those geographic areas? The message may have been sent to those additional area churches as well. Christ's intent was for the message to go to the churches that were developed up to that point in history; therefore, the initial seven churches would be the initial method to distribute the message. Christ knew that as the churches expanded, the message would expand and eventually end up in Scripture which would be carried throughout the world. The same concept can be applied to many of Paul's letters. The book of Ephesians was for the church in Ephesus, yet it ended up in Scripture and applies to all churches of all time. We have built major doctrines from this message to the church in Ephesus. Ephesians 2:8 states *"For by Grace are we saved through faith, and that not of yourselves, it is the gift of God."* We have built solid doctrine on this Scripture alone, without claiming and rationalizing that this letter was only to the church at Ephesus. Excluding it from appropriate usage to help all people and churches would have been a hindrance to the gospel.

A good summary of the true picture of who Christ is at our new reference point on the time line is:

1. Descriptive of how Jesus should be viewed at this juncture in Scripture. This reference point is before the rapture of the Church and the second coming of Christ.
2. Descriptive of the judge who stands in the midst of the churches and who is qualified, able, and willing to judge the churches and ministers of the Church.

Many readers may spend months on this time line arguing, debating, praying, and fussing over the placement of the reference point. I believe after prayerful consideration you will let Scripture and God's voice to the Church override any prejudices, dogma, and personal feelings. My only request is that you heed the warning of Christ when He stated *"He that hath an ear let him hear what the Spirit is saying to the churches."* He stated this on eight occasions in Revelation chapters 2-3.

Chapter Four

Application and Interpretation of Dreams

Now as for these four young men, God endowed them with knowledge and skill in all sorts of literature and wisdom — and Daniel had insight into all kinds of visions and dreams. ~

~ Daniel 1:17 (NET Bible)

Society often forgives the criminal; it never forgives the dreamer.

~ Oscar Wilde

However, there is a God in heaven who reveals mysteries, and he has made known to King Nebuchadnezzar what will happen in the times to come. The dream and the visions you had while lying on your bed are as follows.

~ Daniel 2:28 (NET Bible)

Hopefully you have read through many of the scriptural dreams described and explained in chapters two and three. I would like to focus this chapter on discussing the scriptural evidences and concepts that are implied about dreams, and apply them to our modern day. If dreams are to be taken as serious as I believe they should, then it is worth the read and study of what God's intent really was, and is, for dreams and visions. I have learned that many people love to read and discuss Scripture and talk about how great God was and potentially can be, yet they never make application of the principles in their lives on a regular basis. For this purpose, I want to invest the time to help people go beyond just thinking that God's Word is always for other people, and other time periods, and hopefully use it for their lives today.

Overview of Applying Dreams for Application Today

Every four years that the Olympics take place, you will find that more and more world records are being broken. Just when people think that a person can't run any faster, swim any faster, or compete any better, we find that another generation of people are breaking the last generation's records. There are two key applications from the Olympics that I would like to share that apply to dreams and visions.

1. **Knowledge increasing.** Every four years you will find out that the Olympians have obtained far more knowledge about their sport and their training methods. The increase in this knowledge is directly proportionate to their ability to continue to break world records.
2. **Taking on the required attributes of other athletes.** All athletes who are serious about their sport and being the leader in their sport have learned some key points about being winners. They know if they are to be winners and compete at a world-class level that they need to learn what the previous world record holders did to accomplish what they want to do. They have found that they need to take on many of the same attributes which include training, dieting, and compete at the same events as their predecessors

did. This dedication to take on the attributes of their predecessors along with new knowledge and a complete dedication is part of their recipe for potential success.

The same type of behavior we observe in athletes applies to the behavior we should have in our spiritual life. This very behavior is vital for any potential spiritual leaders who want to learn to model the Godly saints in Scriptures. Both Jesus and the Apostle Paul challenged the readers of Scripture to become like them.

And what you learned and received and heard and saw in me, do these things. And the God of peace will be with you.

~ Philippians 4:9 (NET Bible)

I tell you the truth, anyone who has faith in me will do what I have been doing. He will do even greater things than these, because I am going to the Father. ~ John 14:12 (NIV)

In addition to challenging us to be like Jesus and Paul, Jesus went on to say that if we would become like them and believe that we could do the same things and even greater things than they did. This is a wonderful challenge that many people unfortunately never take serious.

Now let's compare our Olympic example to our potential to take God at face value. In Daniel 12:4 there is a clear indicator that in the last days of time that knowledge and speed/travel would increase. The reference to speed is in part related to travel. As we approach the return of Christ, the dimension of time is speeding up from many facets. This increase in speed/travel combined with the increase in knowledge on how to better use the dimension of time to travel faster and to more places, makes for a fabulous environment to see things we have never seen before. In other words, knowledge is being compounded over time. This explains why technology and the sports worlds have experienced such exponential growth. The people who have taken their business and sports achievements seriously have literally leveraged this basic and biblical principle. Athletes have capitalized on the use of technological advancements to get from one competition to another to compete, as well as train in different parts of the world. They have accessed information from decades ago to learn how their predecessors trained as well as how some succeeded and failed. Business owners have also capitalized on new technology to make quicker advancements and optimize business results. They have also accessed data and information in different ways to determine how to be more efficient and successful by monitoring successes and failures from their financial predecessors.

Somewhere along God's time line He has increased knowledge and sped up time and travel. Unfortunately, it appears that religious folks decided to take a vacation and/or think that this spiritual truth only applies to athletes and the business world. Satan has done a masterful job keeping many Christians from accessing the same increases in revelation and increase in time. Even though Christ promised we could have the keys to the kingdom, many people never learned the secret that the keys to the kingdom included the key to many spiritual rooms as well as an increase in knowledge in the spiritual realm.

Many have sat back and watched the secular world far surpass last year's accomplishments while they dogmatically stood on their one piece of spiritual knowledge for years. The Church and Christians have also gotten so sidetracked trying to finger-point at the world that they forgot it was God's increase in knowledge that would really make the difference within Christianity. Imagine if Christians would have learned from all the past seasons of spiritual harvest(s). They could take both the successes and failures and prepare as well as become more focused on how to speed up and broaden the spiritual revelations, harvest, and growth within the Kingdom. The message of salvation did not have to change to accommodate this, rather the means and manner in which we get the message delivered. When God said that knowledge and time would speed up in the last days (Daniel 12:4), He meant it for sports, business, and all of creation, but most of all for Christianity. Christians are the least excused to fulfill God's spiritual principles which apply to all of creation ... so Lord bring on the revelation and knowledge that you promised that we might catch up to your plan!

> **When God said that knowledge and time would speed up in the last days (Daniel 12:4), He meant it for sports, business, and all of creation, but most of all for Christianity. Christians are the**

least excused to fulfill God's spiritual principles which apply to all of creation ... so Lord bring on the revelation and knowledge that you promised that we might catch up to your plan!

Taking these few principles into the realm of dreams, let's draw some applicable conclusions. The first thing we must look at is the ridiculous nature of any spiritual parent or grandparent who somehow wanted their children to be like many of the biblical characters in the Bible. They spent years praying and hoping that this would be the case. Unfortunately, the change and hope in their children were not going to occur until the children took on many of the attributes of these spiritual people. Many good parents sent their children off to church and Sunday school where they heard many of the stories, but were never encouraged to take on the same attributes that these Bible characters had taken on. Again, it's great to hear the stories but quite another thing to live the same type of stories in our modern day. In essence, there was a lot of talking, sitting, and even praying about this hope for their children, but very little action taken.

Imagine with me that 100 grandparents and parents want their child to be the next gold medalists in swimming, let's say like Michael Phelps. We would all have to admit that these children would have to immediately take on some of the same attributes as Michael Phelps. They would have to trained like he was trained, learn like he learned, eat like he ate, be dedicated like he was dedicated, train against other Olympic hopefuls like he did, etc. We would all agree that joining the YMCA or doing a few laps in the Olympic size pool during the summer would not produce the same results. In the end, these children may be lucky to win one school-wide swim meet. This being said, if I as a parent or grandparent desire my children to be the next Daniel, Naomi, Ruth, David, Job, Paul, Luke, John, Samuel, Joseph, or Mary then my children will have to take on some of the same attributes as these people. They will have to learn about them, study like they studied, be as committed as they were committed, trust like they trusted, have faith like they had faith, suffer like they suffered, and *most of all dream like they dreamed*. As you have found out, many of these very people dreamed, but more importantly they carried out their dreams, and it literally influenced their lives as well as the kingdom of God. If I want to experience and see the things that Daniel saw, then I should do the things that Daniel did, including dreaming and living out my dreams.

> *If I want to see the things that Daniel saw, then I should do the things that Daniel did, including dreaming and living out my dreams.*
>
> ~ Michael L. Mathews

Imagine with me if the last 20 years of Christianity would have advanced at the same rate as the technological, sports, and business world, simply because we believed God's spiritual principle applies to everyone and everything. Imagine with me that in that same 20 years of Christianity we would have included 20 million Christians who each produced a child like a Daniel, Joseph, Ruth, Esther, and others, who believed that God gave dreams and that dreams were meant to be lived out. What we would have seen is exponential and phenomenal growth in the Kingdom that would have put the secular world to shame.

> *Imagine the results of the last 20 years of Christianity if Christians would have advanced at the same rate as the technological, business, and sports world, simply because we believed that God's spiritual principles applied to everyone and everything.*

All this said, the kingdom of God could and should be advancing at a faster rate with more knowledge and quicker results that are far superior to the sports and business world. Many of us have not taken the spiritual world more serious than the sports and business world.

Let me immediately issue an apology to every grandparent or parent who has produced a Daniel, Joseph, Ruth, or Esther and encouraged them to take on the same type of attributes as these godly people. However, I am going to guess that many of the grandparents and parents reading this book have never asked their children about their dreams, passions, visions, and how well they are living out those dreams, passions, and/or visions. Instead, many of these same parents have scolded and insulted their kids by using words that squash or kill every little attempt that could have been the beginning of a godly dream. These words or phrases have included:

1) What were you thinking?
2) You should have known better!!
3) I knew you would amount to no good!
4) You should have been careful!
5) What else did you expect to happen?
6) You're just like your mother, or just like or father!

There is no doubt that there needs to be a balance between protecting our children and encouraging our children. I do believe that there is quite a bit of room for error on the side of encouragement. I believe that many young people have had dreams and visions that went unrealized because no one was there to help push them forward with encouragement. In fact many elderly people will openly admit that many times they missed their dream and vision as what appeared more normal overshadowed their dreams and visions that risked being laughed at. Let's encourage people to dream and vision great and impossible things and then help them fulfill them.

Should Dreams Be Taken More Seriously?

As you have read in chapters two and three, there are numerous biblical cases of people who had dreams and visions. In Scripture the word *dream* is used over 160 times and there are over 25 documented cases of key Biblical characters that had significant dreams that changed lives, nations, and societies. In addition if you combined dreams and visions there are well over 250 applications of dreams and/or visions.

What is interesting is that these dreams are not just conversation pieces; they are real-life experiences that God used to change, protect, and guide not only people put generations as well as societies. Some people may say that 25 cases are not enough to validate that God desires to uses dreams in a serious and significant manner. Consider the 160 references to dreams and visions compared to the less than 2 references concerning musical choirs in Scripture. Because there are only 2 references to choirs, do we assume God does not want us to have musical choirs or sing every Sunday? Consider that there are less than 10 references to people being resurrected from the dead! Do we assume that we should not teach that God has planned for people to be resurrected when He returns? You get my point!

If every church across the world grandstands and platforms musical choirs every week and never encourages dreams or visions, let's just say there is an imbalance in what our efforts and attentions are focused on. I must be honest and compare the results of music and dreams and visions. I wish I could say that Scripture indicates that music and choirs and music ministers would save souls and change nations, but the reality is they can't. If music could save souls, the world would have been won hundreds of years ago, simply based on the amount of focus we place on music and talent. What I can say is ... dreams and visions have changed societies and saved the lives of countless billions. When the power of one dream guides Joseph and Mary to protect the Savior, then we have billions saved! When the power of one dream that Peter had allows all Gentiles into the plan of salvation, then we have billions saved as well. Truly we need to pay attention to dreams and visions.

I realize that music is containable, understandable and controllable, and thus every church emphasizes its importance and necessity. On the other hand, dreams and visions are not containable, not always understandable, and definitely not controllable; therefore, we minimize their importance, and often just ignore them as vital to Christianity. We all need to be reminded that God has blessed people's lives and provided supernatural direction to people for centuries through dreams and visions. That same God desires to utilize dreams in my life and your life. As stated in chapter one, God's desires for the dreams and visions is to help bring people to God's spiritual level. Without dreams and visions, people would seldom, if ever, step out beyond their own personal human limitations. Dreams and visions challenge people to move out into the heavens, or at least goes against their normal comprehension.

General applications and observations about dreams and visions

As stated, there are more than 25 recorded events of people who had significant dreams. Based on these 25 recorded events there are some clear applications and observations that can be made to help you understand how significant and important dreams are.

Applications and Observations:

1. **You must follow through with your dreams and visions.** Because dreams are God's supernatural way of communicating with us to achieve something different than the norm, it stands to reason that people must have faith to do something with their dreams. I believe many people ignore or dismiss their dreams because they do not want to be challenged with the reality of what it takes to fulfill or walk out the dream and/or vision that God gave them. See two examples below:
   i. In the case of the apostle Peter who had the vision we discussed back in chapters 1 and 3, he had a supernatural vision that allowed Gentiles to be accepted into the plan of salvation. This all sounds neat and tidy, but the reality was that Peter had to walk out the dream and do some brave things once he had the dream. In addition to Peter going to Cornelius' house, he had to go to the church council in Jerusalem and tell them how through a vision on a rooftop and a visit to a Gentile's house that all of Christianity was to be changed. You can imagine the doubt and concerns Peter had on his way to the council. I believe he had to be absolutely convinced that the vision was of God. He also had to be extremely convincing about the meaning of the vision. As we know, he followed through on the vision and Christianity was changed forever. What if he would have ignored the vision? What have you done with your dreams and visions?
   ii. The founder of Light for the Lost, Sam Cochran, was an insurance consultant who had a vision of people from every race reaching to heaven for the message of hope. After having the vision/dream Sam asked a minister

what the dream meant, and the minister replied with a basic *"It depends what you do with the vision."* Shortly after the vision (1953), Sam Cochrane and three others started the Light for the Lost ministry which has now raised more that $216,000,000 for literature that spreads the gospel of Hope. The minister made a very profound statement that held much truth. It is not so much our dreams or visions that matter. What matters is if we follow through with them. This is what determines what the dream meant. Have you ever done anything with any of the dreams or visions you have had? I assume the answer to this question is found by determining if you believe your dreams and visions mean anything.

I have questioned whether or not we are supposed to dream as much as we do. I am not absolutely certain how frequent people did dream in Scripture and even if they were all recorded or not recorded. We will never know until we get to heaven. However, I do believe that people may have continual dreams and more frequent dreams when they are always ignoring the dream. When godly people in Scripture struggled with accepting the meaning of a dream or vision, we find that God gave the dream or vision more than once — often three times. After the repeated dream was accepted, the dream appeared to stop. Therefore we may surmise that a dream may be continually repeated at times to get our attention and see if we will respond.

2. **Dreams generally have serious consequences.** Most of the dreams in Scripture have very serious benefits and consequences. We do not see the dreams and visions in Scripture that are "niceties," or dreams that give warm and fuzzy images of angels blowing kisses to humanity. The reason may be as simple as: God gives the dreams and visions to allow His supernatural abilities to intervene in the affairs of man, which is no light and/or inconsequential

matter. We need to keep in mind that the Bible keeps a recording of all the dreams by the characters represented in Scripture. Imagine what would have happened to history and Christianity if many of these recorded dreams were not taken seriously and actually carried out by these men and women of faith. We should not assume that all the recorded dreams are the only ones that took place. Rather, we should assume that God lives up to his written word and many people had significant dreams, but they may have ignored them. Now imagine how many people in our day ignore their dreams and visions. Would our world be a better place if dreams and visions were followed through with? What if by faith we actually realized that God wants to touch and change humanity so He continues to speak through dreams and visions which have serious benefits and consequences. What if many of the dreams we have are really God's creative way of trying to express His concerns in many different manners to get our attention?

It is true that many of us live in very sheltered and limited mindsets that disallow us to see outside our own beliefs. Scientists know that during dreams and visions our minds have a greater capacity for being creative. The reason is that all boundaries in sleep are generally cut off, and our mind is able to see and experience things that our daily minds would never accept. Considering the fact that God is wiser than scientists, we can assume He knows that if He is ever to get us to think outside of our religious boundaries, he will need to do so in the evening hours and/or in visions when our minds are not setting boundaries.

3. **Dream interpretation.** It is clear in Scripture that God gave people the ability to interpret dreams. Scripture also states that dreams and/or mysteries are revealed by God. The following passages are clear indicators of the capability or ability of people to interpret dreams.

They told him, "We both had dreams, but there is no one to interpret them." Joseph responded, "Don't interpretations belong to God? Tell them to me." Genesis 40:8

When the chief baker saw that the interpretation of the first dream was favorable, he said to Joseph, "I also appeared in my dream and there were three baskets of white bread on my head." Genesis 40:16

Now a young man, a Hebrew, a servant of the captain of the guards, was with us there. We told him our dreams, and he interpreted the meaning of each of our respective dreams for us. Genesis 41:12

"Pharaoh said to Joseph, "I had a dream, and there is no one who can interpret it. But I have heard about you, that you can interpret dreams." Genesis 41:15

As for me, this mystery was revealed to me not because I possess more wisdom than any other living person, but so that the king may understand the interpretation and comprehend the thoughts of your mind. Daniel 2:30

You saw that a stone was cut from a mountain, but not by human hands; it smashed the iron, bronze, clay, silver, and gold into pieces. The great God has made known to the king what will occur in the future. The dream is certain, and its interpretation is reliable. Daniel 2:45

Saying, "Belteshazzar, chief of the magicians, in whom I know there to be a spirit of the holy gods and whom no mystery baffles, consider my dream that I saw and set forth its interpretation! Daniel 4:9

"This is the dream that I, King Nebuchadnezzar, saw. Now you, Belteshazzar, declare its interpretation, for none of the wise men in my kingdom are able to make known to me the interpretation. But you can do so, for a spirit of the holy gods is in you." Daniel 4:18

Then Daniel (whose name is also Belteshazzar) was upset for a brief time; his thoughts were alarming him. The king said, "Belteshazzar, don't let the dream and its interpretation alarm you." But

Belteshazzar replied, "Sir, if only the dream were for your enemies and its interpretation applied to your adversaries!" Daniel 4:19

"Thus there was found in this man Daniel, whom the king renamed Belteshazzar, an extraordinary spirit, knowledge, and skill to interpret dreams, solve riddles, and decipher knotty problems. Now summon Daniel, and he will disclose the interpretation." Daniel 5:12

"However, I have heard that you are able to provide interpretations and to decipher knotty problems. Now if you are able to read this writing and make known to me its interpretation, you will wear purple and have a golden collar around your neck and be third ruler in the kingdom." Daniel 5:16

I approached one of those standing nearby and asked him about the meaning of all this. So he spoke with me and revealed to me the interpretation of the vision. Daniel 7:16

Gideon arrived just as a man was telling a friend his dream. "I had a dream," he was saying. "A round loaf of barley bread came tumbling into the Midianite camp. It struck the tent with such force that the tent overturned and collapsed."

His friend responded, "This can be nothing other than the sword of Gideon son of Joash, the Israelite. God has given the Midianites and the whole camp into his hands."

When Gideon heard the dream and its interpretation, he worshiped God. He returned to the camp of Israel and called out, "Get up! The LORD has given the Midianite camp into your hands." Dividing the three hundred men into three companies, he placed trumpets and empty jars in the hands of all of them, with torches inside. Judges 7:13-16 (NIV)

But the angel said to me, "Why are you astounded? I will interpret for you the mystery of the woman and of the beast with the seven heads and ten horns that carries her. Revelation 17:7 (NET Bible)

It needs to be stated that the Bible does not indicate that dream interpretation is one of the gifts of the Spirit. However God does state that people do receive His revelations when dreams are given. Because God is not in the business of giving dreams without some sort of revelation, He may require that we seek, ask and knock (Luke 11:9-10) to determine the message. Many times the interpretations are received after seeking the meaning by the very person who had the dream. At other times, depending on the spiritual level of the person having the dream, or the ability to have a clear mind at a specific time, the ability to interpret the dream on your own is hampered. God may have us ask other people to use their ability to give the revelation/interpretation, when we are not capable.

When looking in Scripture it is clear that many of the recorded dreams and visions were easily interpreted by the person having the dream or vision. There are other cases where the dream was so futuristic or complex that there was only one person found who could interpret. This was the very case with Joseph and Daniel. God gifted them with wisdom and no one else in their day could interpret the complex dreams that the kings of their day had. Lastly, Daniel had dreams that were so futuristic that the Lord informed him that the dreams were meant for a future day revelation.

When we look at the dreams of Nebuchadnezzar and Pharaoh and the reality that no one except Joseph and Daniel could interpret the dreams, a few key points need to be made. It is possible that the dream could not be interpreted out of fear of 1) the magnitude or impact of the dream; and/or 2) the panic caused by Kings; and 3) the fear of not being accurate with the dream. If you go back and read about these dreams it is evident that the times and demands of the kings who had the dreams were challenging. The interpretation of these kinds of dreams may cost a person their life.

Considering these points, we really need to step back and ask about the time we are presently living in as a way to understand why or why not people can interpret their own dreams. Most people realize that the times we live in are very perplexing, and many people are riddled by fear. This fear generally rattles people's faith and good common spiritual sense. This type of environment makes it extremely difficult to be spiritually astute and sharp in godly wisdom. I have even heard solid pastors recently state in different words: *"By the time the words of Scripture leave my lips and hit the congregation's ears; the words have been distorted."* They are saying this because they can see the intent of their heart and God's words are causing confusion in the people's eyes, or instant disagreement because the words are being misunderstood.

This perplexing time we live in may also explain why people — including good solid individuals and ministers alike are doing what normally would be unthinkable. The times are creating a form of confusion in people's minds which may be caused by fear, worry, and doubt because of what they are experiencing. This said, it should stand to reason that dreams may 1) appear more complicated because our lives are more complicated; and 2) not all people are in the right frame of mind to interpret their dreams.

This may help explain why many people are simply ignoring their dreams. I have found that in my life, when I have been extremely stressed, or caught up in a fearful moment, that my mind does not want to process certain things that appear to add to my stress, or simply put, my mind cannot handle any more thoughts. I believe that the present situation in the world has produced more frequent and longer periods of stress. This increase in frequency and longer durations of frustration, fear, and/or stress surely will inhibit people from processing average day-to-day information, let alone semi-convoluted dreams. Unfortunately, the two appear to work against each other in the sense that during times of uncertainty and/or information overload is the time we will dream. Our minds and brains as stated earlier are recalibrating all the information that we could process during the day. In addition, the fear and uncertainty will affect how we interpret the dreams. The adage, "Sometimes we are so far in the forest that we have bark marks on our forehead" is more common and applicable than we think.

I believe this is the reason God is giving more people the ability to help other individuals understand their dreams. It is fair to say that even though the world and my circumstances may be overwhelming, God still desires to speak to me. Whether I understand the dream or not is irrelevant. I need to understand that if God was ever concerned with my situation and wanted to help me, it is during the times of difficulty, thus He will give me dreams and visions to overcompensate for my negative situations. The question is, will I seek the signs and information He is giving through asking, seeking, knocking in prayer, and other people who are not stressed out at the time, who can help interpret my dream? It is amazing how many people in life will see a sign for their favorite restaurant on the highway and not stop looking until they find it. They will even circle around until they find the place all because they saw the sign. What if each of us would seek the end result of the signs God gives us through dreams and visions?

> *It is amazing how many people in life will see a sign for their favorite restaurant on the highway and not stop until they find it, all because they saw the sign; but they will never seek the sign from God through a dream or vision.*
>
> ~ Michael L. Mathews

Based on the dreams that have been interpreted in Scripture it should be easy to surmise that God gives the ability and wisdom for people to interpret dreams. This is especially true during times of difficulty and moments when people cannot think clearly. I personally believe that in general, we have made dreams far more complicated than what we should. I say this based on the fact that God gives dreams to help people and get them on a straight path (Job 33:14-18). When the general reason for having dreams is clearly understood, wisdom can be applied to the purpose and the interpretation of the dream.

By reviewing the dreams in Scripture, it becomes clear that the majority of dreams given to godly people were immediately interpreted. This implies once again the probability that dreams are not intended to be difficult. On the other hand, the dreams that were given to people who were struggling with their relationship with God, needed to have someone interpret the dreams for them, a godly person with wisdom. Keep in mind, this is an observation and not to be an absolute fact that should cause concern if you do not immediately understand your dream.

Even though dreams are meant to be simpler than we make them, the very fact that they are from God causes us to think they are more difficult. This is especially true for people who think or believe that God is unapproachable, or completely off from their radar screen. The more confusion and/or the more distant we are from God, the more unlikely the interpretation of a dream will be. A clear mind allows wisdom to flow and finds ways to get connected with God's spoken words through a dream.

4. **Our dreams take on our experience and personality.** It is amazing as you listen to people's dreams and learn of the various ways that God uses our minds and experiences. This variety includes extremely hilarious events, simple thoughts combined with perplexing thoughts, life, death, laughter, sorrow, and our relationships with other people. In essence, dreams represent all the facets of our life including our experiences, background, and upbringing.

We can learn from scriptural dreams that God has a sense of humor and has a great sense of creativity. The dream recorded in Scripture (Genesis 31) concerning Jacob's opportunity to become wealthy is a wonderful example of God's creativity. God tells Jacob to make a deal with his abusive boss. The deal was that from that day forward Jacob gets all the impure sheep, and his boss gets the pure sheep. The impure sheep are defined as all the striped, speckled, or spotted, and the pure sheep are defined as all the pure-colored sheep. Within this dream God tells Jacob how to miraculously produce spotted, speckled and striped sheep. He was to peel back the bark on tree branches and put them in front of the sheep as they came to feed and breed. This power of suggestion while feeding and breeding caused them to miraculously produce offspring that were speckled, spotted or striped. In Jacob's dream God used Jacob's personality of "making deals" as well "laboring for a living." God also used Jacob's surroundings and experience of working as a shepherd. Jacob somehow related to the dream and followed out the dream perfectly.

Dreams follow our experiences.

As Job was going through his trials he made a very significant observation about dreams. The observation was that dreams reflect the real life you are living. During part of Job's life he was experiencing numerous impossible circumstances. In essence what he says is, "*As soon as I think I can lie down on a couch or bed and rest from my problems, then the dreams and visions scare and terrify me.*" The exact verse in the NIV is: "When I think my bed will comfort me and my couch will ease my complaint, even then you frighten me with dreams and terrify me with visions" (Job 7:1).

What he is saying is important to us. Our dreams do reflect the life we are living, and track how we perceive things at a given point in time. In Job's case, because he was experiencing difficulties that are hard to fathom, it would be hard for him to have dreams of comfort. In essence, his dreams were following the reality of where he was at in life during that time.

Scientists have concluded that dreams are real, and that dreams directly correlate to our experiences. A person who has experienced the best that life has to offer with little fears or worries, will more than likely have dreams that are on the sweeter side of life. In the same manner, a person who is under tremendous pressure will generally dream about stressful things. Again, I am making a general statement, and there are exceptions as God intervenes in our dreams to produce a new direction or provide encouragement.

Dreams should help solve problems!

What we need to realize is that dreams are intended to help us and provide answers. This means that during difficult circumstances, I may initially dream fearful thoughts. What I should do is turn this around and ask God to help me allow the dreams to provide an answer to my circumstance. Many people cannot do that because the fear within stops them from seeking an answer. We can go to bed and ask the question, how can I remove the stress or solve the circumstance? You may be surprised how your mind in sleep will be open to solutions versus just the reminder of the problems. This is why people who have a specific problem and a few possible solutions in which a decision needs to be made say, "Let me sleep on it." The next day they feel much better about the solution. The reason is simply that they went to bed with the possible solutions on their mind. During the evening their mind processes all solutions and allows the best one to surface. This is in part because the mind was not under pressure or a timetable.

It is amazing to hear from people who are having dreams and find out that many aspects in their dreams are a reflection of what kind of occupation they have had or have. For instance:

- I can talk to military personnel, and a lot of their dreams include military settings, because that is where life was probably the most impressionable.
- I could talk to an athlete and find that most of their dreams involve sports and or competitive situations.
- I could talk to a homemaker or mother and find that most of their dreams involve a nurturing aspect of life.

- I can talk to a person who has had their spouse have an adulterous affair and find that their dreams may involve around unhealthy relationships and/or distrust.

Test this concept by talking to a few people about their dreams, and you will find that a good portion of their dream life includes a setting that involves their day-to-day life or impressionable experiences in their life. It is important to realize that just because the atmosphere in the dream is like their life experiences, one should not conclude that it has anything to do with the meaning of their dream. The setting of a dream is much like the setting of our workplace or home in that the setting of our workplace or home does not define the meaning of what happens to us every day. The setting brings comfort and familiarity, but the details around the setting define outcomes. So, when thinking about the meaning of dreams it is important to pay attention to the details and or significant things around the setting, versus the setting.

In summary, we should not be afraid of dreams or ignore our dreams. Rather, we should work on taking full advantage of our minds during the day as well as the evening. Just because we are sleeping we should not give over our minds and be ignorant of what happens in the evening hours. God desires that we worship Him with all our hearts and all our minds. We need to leverage the fact that God uses dreams and visions to expand our minds. This simply means that He gives us special guidance, help, and answers to questions when our minds are recalibrating or relaxed in the evening hours. He knows that our minds are more available during the evening hours and that the daily boundaries we place on our minds are not active during the night. During the day many of us immediately come up with 10 "Why not?" or "It won't work" scenarios for every opportunity that comes along. In the evening, your mind is not coming up with the negative why not scenarios, but actually working from all possibilities which include things we missed during the day. We serve an awesome God!

Chapter Five

Scientifically Speaking

If one advances confidently in the direction of his dreams, and endeavors to live the life which he has imagined, he will meet with a success unexpected in common hours.

~ Henry David Thoreau

I will bless the Lord who has counseled me; Indeed, my mind [inner man] instructs me in the night.

~ Psalm 16:7 (NASB)

It should be noted up front in this chapter that the intent of this book is not to scientifically prove dreams; but rather to explain the truth that God choose to use dreams. Nonetheless, it is important for people to understand some basic fundamentals of dreams so they can quickly see how God's use of dreams and scientific research closely align with the reality of dreams. There are many fine resources that give scientific evidence of dreams as well as much more in-depth studies as to details on interpreting dreams.

The basic aspects of dreams

Scientific studies have proven two basic yet key aspects of humans during their sleep.

1. Their minds are active
2. They dream

The fact that human minds are active and that they dream should help us realize that dreaming is not weird, but more natural than we think. Considering that both scientists confirm, and God states that we will dream should give you a new-found appreciation for paying attention to what is happening to your mind while you are sleeping.

As a good thinking individual, I should be curious and interested in what my mind is processing during the evening hours. If I am to serve God with all my heart and mind, then I need to be aware of the aspect of my mind in the sleeping hours. For this reason, many methods for recording and journaling dreams have been created. Again, my attempt is to get you to believe in the reality and significance of dreams and not create a method.

The Basics of Sleep and Dream Cycles

It has long been known that sleep is governed by the balance between two opposed brain circuits, one of which produces transmitter chemicals that promote sleep, and the other chemicals that inhibit it.

The circuits are locked in continuous see-saw tussle with one another. Depending on which has gained the upper hand, the brain is switched from sleep to wakefulness and back again.

Although sleep may appear to be a steady state, it actually is made up of numerous stages that cycle throughout your sleep at night. The types of brain activity or brain waves present at different times of the night determine the stage of sleep a person is experiencing. The types of brain waves can be thought of as stages of sleep or stages of brain activity. The most vivid type of dreams referred to as lucid dreams occur in the 5th stage of sleep, known as the REM (Rapid Eye Moment) stage. As the name REM implies, this stage has the most profound discernible characteristic of activity or bursts of rapid eye movement while dreaming. Although dreaming occurs during the other stages of sleep, the most vivid dreaming occurs during this stage.

One complete sleep cycle or stage lasts about 1½ hours; therefore during an average sleep period a person will experience 4 to 5 complete sleep cycles. The sleep cycle starts with four stages of SWS (Slow-Wave Sleep), also referred to as NREM (Non-REM). Many scientists believe that after the completion of the 4th stage, the 5th stage does not immediately begin; instead, the first 4 stages quickly reverse and are then immediately followed by a REM stage of sleep. The first REM period will occur roughly 1½ hours after falling asleep; thus the first REM stage will last about 10 minutes, given the length of each sleep cycle being roughly 100 minutes. The length of the stages is not static, however: as the night proceeds, the length of stages 3 and 4 (also called delta or deep sleep) begins to fade, and the length of REM stage starts to increases. The REM stage increases up to about one hour in length after a number of sleep cycles have occurred. This process of cycles indicates that as the night goes on, you will dream for longer periods of time.

The following table, showing frequency in minutes, offers a summary of the stages of sleep:

Stage of Sleep	Brain Waves		Common Characteristics
	Frequency	Type	
Stage 1 Slow Wave (Non-REM)	4 to 8	alpha, theta	<ul><li>transition state between sleep and wakefulness</li><li>eyes begin to roll slightly</li><li>consists mostly of theta waves (high amplitude, low frequency (slow))</li><li>brief periods of alpha waves, similar to those present while awake</li><li>lasts only for a few minutes before moving on to next stage</li><li>also referred to as hypnagogia stage</li></ul>
Stage 2 Slow Wave (Non-REM)	8 to 15	theta, spindles, k-complexes	<ul><li>peaks of brain waves become higher and higher (*sleep spindles*)</li><li>*k-complexes* (peaks suddenly, drastically descends, and then picks back up) follow spindles</li><li>again, only lasts for a few minutes</li></ul>
Stage 3 Slow Wave (Non-REM)	2 to 4	delta, theta	<ul><li>also called delta sleep or deep sleep</li><li>very slow brain waves, called delta waves (lower frequency than theta waves)</li><li>20 to 50% of brain waves are delta waves; the rest are theta waves</li></ul>
Stage 4 Slow Wave (Non-REM)	0.5 to 2	delta, theta	<ul><li>again, also called delta sleep or deep sleep</li><li>more than 50% of brain waves are delta waves; the rest are theta waves</li><li>last (and deepest) of the sleep stages before REM sleep; stages reverse and then REM sleep begins</li></ul>
Stage 5 (REM)	> 12	beta	<ul><li>beta waves have a high frequency and occur when the brain is quite active, both in REM sleep and while awake</li><li>frequent bursts of rapid eye movement, along with occasional muscular twitches</li><li>heart may beat faster, and breathing may become shallow and rapid</li><li>most vivid dreaming occurs during this stage</li><li>also known as the paradoxical stage</li></ul>

The Recent History of Dream Understanding

It should be understood that dreams have been studied for centuries, and just as in any other area of science, more information and knowledge is being discovered. In this section it is my desire to share what modern history shares about dreams so the reader can see many viewpoints, yet understand that dreams are an essential part of our lives and we should take them more seriously. The information will be at a higher level and fairly broad.

In 1953, Eugene Aserinsky of the University of Chicago noticed that the eyes of sleeping babies moved beneath their eyelids at certain regular intervals. This led to the discovery of REM (Rapid Eye Movement) sleep periods, which occur at roughly 90 minute intervals throughout the night and which contain the dreams which are the most vivid and most frequently recalled in our memory. Since then, EEG (electroencephalogram) recordings, which monitor brain activity during sleep, have been used to map the various stages of sleep. These states are classified roughly into sleep onset (hypnagogia or stage 1), non-REM sleep (deep sleep or stages 2, 3, and 4), and REM (or paradoxical) sleep.

Eugene Aserinsky's discovery has assisted other scientists to determine that it is within the dream world that small babies and children dream of themselves walking, talking, and learning the basics of life. Even though the day for babies is filled with observing parents walk and talk, the nighttime dreams allow them to envision the things that seem impossible during the daytime hours. This begs the question; "What if we all leaned on the dream process to help us envision the impossible?" It is possible that the dream world allows individuals to escape the traditional narrow mind view with all the standard fears and worries that hinder us from using our imagination and creativity. In the evening hours there are much less limitations on our minds, than what we put around our minds during the day. This would definitely explain why God has given many creative solutions to people in dreams. This also explains why many people have had creative inventions during dreams in the evening.

REM (Paradoxical) Sleep

REM sleep is distinguishable from NREM sleep by changes in physiological states, including its characteristic rapid eye movements. However, polysomnograms show wave patterns in REM to be similar to Stage 1 sleep. In normal sleep (in people without disorders of sleep-wake patterns or REM behavior disorder), heart rate and respiration speed up and become erratic, while the face, fingers, and legs may twitch. Intense dreaming occurs during REM sleep as a result of heightened cerebral activity, but paralysis occurs simultaneously in the major voluntary muscle groups, including the submental muscles (muscles of the chin and neck).

Because REM is a mixture of encephalic (brain) states of excitement and muscular immobility, it is sometimes called paradoxical sleep. It is generally thought that REM-associated muscle paralysis is meant to keep the body from acting out the dreams that occur during this intensely cerebral stage. The first period of REM typically lasts 10 minutes, with each recurring REM stage lengthening, and the final one lasting an hour.

Lucid Dreaming

Although science has proven that everyone dreams every night, many people often remember no dreams at all, and even when they do, it is almost exclusively upon awakening, or after the fact that some people remember their dreams. No matter how much we try and explain away dreams or the fact we have them, the reality is people dream, and God instituted them. This does not negate the fact that just as Satan and evil minds control certain thoughts in our mind in daytime hours, they can do the same in evening hours. This is one of the many reasons why we need to take total control of our mind and know what is happening in it at all times.

Lucid dreams are uniquely different. This type of dreaming during (REM) is when a person realizes that one is dreaming while the dream is still happening. During this stage the dream expands in vividness and clarity as the dreamer becomes aware that the setting that they are experiencing, although appearing very believable, is really a dream and that his or her physical body is elsewhere safe asleep in bed. Many people believe that the lucid dreamer is free to explore remarkable worlds limited only by imagination, and not just as an actor, but also to some degree as a producer and director.

Lucid dreaming was brought into the academic and public spotlights around the world once it's scientific validity was separately proven by researchers at Stanford University, California (where it has also been proven to be a learnable skill), and at Liverpool University, England. Proof was achieved by performing, during REM sleep, a series of extreme left-right eye signals which were agreed upon prior to sleep. Though most of the body's muscles are de-activated during REM sleep, the eye muscles are not, and repeated experiments at Stanford, the Sacré-Coeur Hospital Dream and Nightmare Laboratory and elsewhere have proven that the eyes (and to some extent other physiological responses) can be brought under conscious control by a dreamer who realizes that he or she is dreaming.

Modern-Day Examples Where Dreams Helped Society

1. <u>Paul Tholey</u> was a German psychologist and lucid dream researcher who used dream work in his training of the German Olympic ski jumping team. He had the skiers learn lucid dreaming so that they could creatively experiment with new maneuvers, without risk of injury, and gain confidence in the most believable virtual environment available — the world of dreams.
2. <u>Srinivasa Ramanujan</u> was one of India's greatest mathematical geniuses. He made substantial contributions to analytical theory of numbers and worked on elliptical functions, continued fractions, and infinite series. Despite the lack of a university education, he became known in the Madras area in 1911 after the publication of a brilliant paper on Bernoulli numbers in 1911. In 1914, he was invited in to Cambridge University by the English mathematician GH Hardy who recognized his unconventional genius. He worked there for five years producing startling results. According to Ramanujan, inspiration and insight for his

work came to him in his dreams. A Hindu goddess, named Namakkal, would appear and present mathematical formulae which he would verify after waking. Such dreams often repeated themselves, and the connection with the dream world as a source for his work was constant throughout his life.

3. <u>Jack Nicklaus</u> In 1964, after an embarrassing slump, golfer Jack Nicklaus claims to have solved a problem with his golf swing within a dream, which subsequently improved his game by ten strokes — overnight!

4. <u>Friedrich August Kekule</u> who discovered the structure of benzene reported the following dream:

> "Again the atoms were juggling before my eyes ... my mind's eye, sharpened by repeated sights of a similar kind, I could now distinguish larger structures of different forms and in long chains, many of them close together; everything was moving in a snake-like and twisting manner. Suddenly, what was this? One of the snakes got hold of its own tail and the whole structure was mockingly twisting in front of my eyes. As if stuck by lightening I awoke ..."

This dream led Kekule to the realization that the structure of benzene is a closed carbon ring with an atom of carbon and hydrogen at each point of a hexagon. His discovery revolutionized the field of organic chemistry. When Kekule recounted his dream to his colleagues at a scientific convention in 1890, he concluded with the remarks "Let us learn to dream gentlemen and then we may perhaps find the truth."

5. <u>Elias Howe</u> invented the sewing machine in 1845. Howe started working on his design for a sewing machine in 1840. He had the idea of a machine with a needle which would go through a piece of cloth but he couldn't figure out exactly how it would work. He first tried using a needle that was pointed at both ends, with an eye in the middle, but it was a failure. Then one night he had a nightmare. He

dreamed he was a missionary taken prisoner by a group of natives. They were dancing around him with spears. As he saw them move around him, his attention was drawn to their spears. They all had holes near their tips. When he woke up he realized that the dream had brought the solution to his problem. By locating a hole at the tip of the needle, the thread could be caught after it went through cloth thus making his machine operable. He changed his design to incorporate the dream idea and found that it worked.

6. <u>Louis Agassiz</u> was a Swiss-born naturalist, geologist, and teacher who immigrated to the US in 1846. He made revolutionary contributions to natural science with landmark work on glacier activity and extinct fishes. He trained and influenced a generation of American zoologists and paleontologists and is one of the founding fathers of the modern American scientific tradition.

While Agassiz was working on his vast work "Poissons Fossiles" a list of all know fossil fish, he came across a specimen which he was, at first, unable to figure out. He hesitated to classify it and extract it since an incorrect approach could ruin the specimen. At that time, Agassiz reports having a dream three nights in a row in which he saw the fish in perfect original condition. The first two nights — being unprepared — he did not record his image. By the third night he was ready with pen and paper, and when the fish appeared again in the dream he drew it in the dark, still half asleep. The next day he looked at his drawing which had remarkably different features from the ones he had been working out, hastened to his laboratory, and extracting the fossil, realized it corresponded exactly to his dream.

7. <u>Otto Loewi</u> was a German-born physiologist who won the Nobel Prize in 1938 for his work on the chemical transmission of nerve impulses. In 1903, Loewi had the idea that there might be a chemical transmission of the nervous impulse rather than an electrical one — which was the common-held belief — but he was at a loss on how to

prove it. He let the idea slip to the back of his mind until 17 years later he had the following dream. According to Loewi:

> The night before Easter Sunday of that year I awoke, turned on the light, and jotted down a few notes on a tiny slip of paper. Then I fell asleep again. It occurred to me at 6 o'clock in the morning that during the night I had written down something most important, but I was unable to decipher the scrawl. The next night, at 3 o'clock, the idea returned. It was the design of an experiment to determine whether or not the hypothesis of chemical transmission that I had uttered 17 years ago was correct. I got up immediately, went to the laboratory, and performed a single experiment on a frog's heart according to the nocturnal design.

The result of the experiment became the foundation for the theory of chemical transmission of the nervous impulse.

A View of Dreams by Carl Jung

Carl Jung, a well-known scientist, put forth some very insightful frameworks for understanding the symbolism and nature of dreams, including his concepts of universal personality archetypes and the collective unconscious. Yet Jung himself wrote, "I have no theory about dreams. I do not know how dreams arise. I am altogether in doubt as to whether my way of handling dreams deserves the name "method." But ... if we meditate on a dream sufficiently long and thoroughly ... something almost always comes of it." Jung added that this something is rarely of rational, scientific nature, but rather "a practical and important hint which shows the patient in what direction the unconscious is leading him." Jung observed that dreams perform restorative, corrective, compensatory, prophetic and developmental roles in the psyche and believed that we must be ready at any moment to construct an entirely new theory of dreams.

Dream Recall

Many Christian and non-Christian scholars and organizations have very similar theories on recalling your dreams. I have included the following basic information which summarizes the basic elements.

Simple Practices for Recalling Dreams

1. Believe your dreams are meaningful and important. Your attitude toward dreaming is key. Make a sincere and conscious effort to remember a dream. Practice what many call "auto-suggestion" before going to sleep. As you fall asleep tell yourself: "I'm going to remember my dreams when I wake up."
2. When you first awake, keep your eyes closed. Go over the dream in your mind's eye and remember as much as you can. Don't dismiss small dream fragments or dreams which seem trivial. Thinking about them can bring back a whole night's series. When you remember a dream, rehearse it several times in order to fix it in your memory. If you get up at this point and start your regular activities before reviewing the dream, chances are that many of the details of the dream will vanish.
3. You may find it helpful to keep a notebook and pen beside your bed so you can write notes when you wake up without having to get up. Some people have been known to keep a tape recorder and record their dreams when they awaken.
4. Write down your dreams in the order in which you recall them. Write out as much as you can remember. Don't worry about the meaning of your dreams as you write them down — the important thing is to get them on paper or on your tape recorder. Even if you recall only a single image, record that in as much detail as you can.
5. Some people find it beneficial to give their dream a title. It helps to focus the memory of the dream and can help in understanding it later on. You may also want to create a sketch of your dream or to illustrate in a visual manner with maps or diagrams.

6. You may recall fragments of dreams during the day. If so, write them down. Remembering such pieces can help you recall other dreams. It also helps to cultivate the flow between the dream and waking worlds.

7. Record your emotional feelings relating to your dream. How did you feel about the events within the dream? What mood were you in when you woke up? Did any emotions or experiences from the dream linger on?
8. If you can't remember anything about the dream, write down whatever spontaneous images or thoughts occur to you. Sometimes this can trigger recall, and it also sets a pattern of recording. You can also note descriptions about the night. Did you sleep well or badly? What were your thoughts upon going to sleep or awakening?
9. If you take your dreams seriously, then dream recall will become a habit and a practice. If you regard your dreams as important and cultivate an interest in them, they will come to you more readily and more often.

Frequently Asked Questions About Dreams

There are thousands of questions relating to dreams. In addition, there are numerous resources for further study on dreams from a scientific perspective. Below is a fair summation of some of the basic questions many people have. These frequently asked questions are located on the website of The International Association For the Study of Dreams: http://www.asdreams.org.

Does everyone dream?

Yes. Laboratory studies have shown that we experience our most vivid dreams during a type of sleep called Rapid Eye Movement (REM) sleep. During REM sleep the brain is very active, the eyes move back and forth rapidly under the lids, and the large muscles of the body are relaxed. REM sleep occurs every 90 - 100 minutes, 3 to 4 times a night, and lasts longer as the night progresses. The final REM period may last as long as 45 minutes. Less vivid dreams occur at other times during the night.

Why do people have trouble remembering their dreams?

Some people have no difficulty in remembering several dreams nightly, whereas others recall dreams only occasionally or not at all. Nearly everything that happens during sleep — including dreams, the thoughts which occur throughout the night and memories of brief awakenings — is forgotten by morning. There is something about the phenomenon of sleep itself which makes it difficult to remember what has occurred and most dreams are forgotten unless they are written down. Sometimes a dream is suddenly remembered later in the day or on another day, suggesting that the memory is not totally lost but for some reason is very hard to retrieve. Sleep and dreams also are affected by a great variety of drugs and medications, including alcohol. Further, stopping certain medications suddenly may cause nightmares. It is advisable to discuss with your physician the effect of any drugs or medications you are taking.

How can I improve my dream memory?

Before you fall asleep, remind yourself that you want to remember your dreams. Keep a paper and pen or tape-recorder by your bedside. As you awaken, try to move as little as possible and try not to think right away about your upcoming day. Write down all of your dreams and images, as they can fade quickly if not recorded. Any distractions will cause the memory of your dream to fade. If you can't remember a full dream, record the last thing that was on your mind before awakening, even if you have only a vague memory of it.

Are dreams in color?

Most dreams are in color, although people may not be aware of it, either because they have difficulty remembering their dreams or because color is such a natural part of visual experience. People who are very aware of color while awake probably notice color more often in their dreams.

Do dreams have meaning?

Although scientists continue to debate this issue, most people who work with their dreams, either by themselves or with others, find that their dreams are very meaningful for them. Dreams are useful in learning more about the dreamer's feelings, thoughts, behavior, motives, and values. Many find that dreams can help them solve problems. Further, artists, writers, and scientists often get creative ideas from dreams.

How can I learn to interpret my dreams?

The most important thing to keep in mind is that your dreams reflect your own underlying thoughts and feelings, and that the people, actions, settings and emotions in your dreams are personal to you. Some dream experts theorize that there are typical or archetypal dreams and dream elements that persist across different persons, cultures, and times. Usually, however, the same image or symbol will have different meanings for different people. For example, an elephant in a dream can mean one thing to a zoo keeper and something quite different to a child whose favorite toy is a stuffed elephant. Therefore, books which give a specific meaning for a specific dream image or symbol (or "dream dictionaries") are not usually helpful. By thinking about what each dream element means to you or reminds you of, by looking for parallels between these associations and what is happening in your waking life, and by being patient and persistent, you can learn to understand your dreams. It can be helpful to keep a dream diary and reflect on many dreams over a long period of time to get the truest picture of your unique dream life. Many good books can help you get started interpreting your dreams.

What does it mean when I have the same dream over and over?

Recurrent dreams, which can continue for years, may be treated as any other dream. That is, one may look for parallels between the dream and the thoughts, feelings, behavior, and motives of the dreamer. Understanding the meaning of the recurrent dream sometimes can help the dreamer resolve an issue that he or she has been struggling with for years.

Is it normal to have nightmares?

Nightmares are very common among children and fairly common among adults. Often nightmares are caused by stress, traumatic experiences, emotional difficulties, drugs or medication, or illness. However, some people have frequent nightmares that seem unrelated to their waking lives. Recent studies suggest that these people tend to be more open, sensitive, trusting, and emotional than average.

Is it true that if you dream that you die or that you hit bottom in a falling dream, you will in fact die in your sleep?

No, these beliefs are not true. Many people have dreamed that they died or hit bottom in a fall and they have lived to tell the tale! You can explore the meaning of these kinds of images just as you would explore any others that might occur in your dreams. However, if any aspect of your dreams worries or distresses you, talk to a professional mental health practitioner about your concerns.

Can dreams predict the future?

There are many examples of dreams that seemed to predict future events. Some may have been due to coincidence, faulty memory, or an unconscious tying together of known information. A few laboratory studies have been conducted of predictive dreams, as well as clairvoyant and telepathic dreams, but the results were varied, as these kinds of dreams are difficult to study in a laboratory setting.

Is it possible to control dreams?

You often can influence your dreams by giving yourself pre-sleep suggestions. Another method of influencing dreams is called lucid dreaming, in which you are aware you are dreaming while still asleep and in the dream. Sometimes people experience this type of dreaming spontaneously. It is often possible to learn how to increase lucid dreaming, and thereby increase your capacity to affect the course of the dream events as they unfold. Some things are easier than others to control, and indeed complete control is probably never possible. Some professional dream workers question the advisability of trying to control the dream, and encourage learning to enjoy and understand it instead.

Chapter Six

Samples of Dreams and Interpretation

Dreams are illustrations from the book your soul is writing about you. ~ Marsha Norman

I will bless the Lord who has counseled me; Indeed, my mind (inner man) instructs me in the night.

~ Ps. 16:7 (NASB)

When God stated that all of creation would be waiting for the manifestations of the Sons of God; He specifically declared and proclaimed that all of His people would be used to reveal Him — not just ministers; no one was excluded. It's time for the Church and ministers to release the sons and daughters of God.

~ Michael L. Mathews

The Bible states that dreams are to be understood and/or interpreted. We have covered the reality that many of the people in Scripture were able to understand the meanings of their dreams. Even though they struggled with the dreams, they for the most part understood the meaning. Most dreams can be self-interpreted assuming that the dream is personal and the person dreaming has a clear mind.

> *Most dreams can be self interpreted assuming that the dream is personal and the person dreaming has a clear mind.*
>
> ~ Michael L. Mathews

On the other hand there are some of the Biblical dreams where the dreams were so complex, broad in nature and/or impacting that the person could not comprehend them without God's intervention through another person who had that magnitude of understanding or wisdom.

> *Some dreams are so complex, broad in nature, or impact a society to such a degree that a person cannot comprehend it without God's intervention through another person who had the magnitude of understanding or wisdom.*
>
> ~ Michael L. Mathews

This chapter explores some examples of dreams, along with the interpretation, that have been shared with the author. This is intended to help people see the simplicity of dreams and how God may speak in various ways through the sleep. It is absolutely critical that people are continually reminded that God loves humanity and He uses dreams primarily to help keep them from the Pit or hell as explained in Job 33:14-18. As a person studies dreams and listens to people's dreams you will find that there are many dreams that are fairly similar in descriptions and could be identified as identical messages from God with the exception of some of the characters or environment. This should not be surprising when you consider that God is trying to get a similar message across, just personalizing it.

Dream 1 – Understanding the Harvest

The dreamer (He) owns a large segment of land that people love to use for deer hunting. He also is a deer hunter, and during one particular season everyone asked him for the best locations on the land. After he had given away all the prime locations, all that was left was a spot right at the front of the woods. He settled down patiently in the front of the woods and let the day-long hunt begin. The entire day went by, and no one shot at anything. There were absolutely no shots fired. This was very unusual as the deer population on the property was plentiful. Right before evening, when everyone started coming in from the hunt, they would get about 50 yards from him and suddenly big bucks would jump out 10 feet from his stand. All the hunters would shoot, but he was the only one who could actually kill the deer. The though kept going through his mind in the dream was "they were here all this time, and the deer would not move until the right time."

Interpretation 1:

In the dream the property and deer hunt season represent a (gospel) harvest period. The owner of the land was a gracious person who always helped people and gave away some of the best parts and pieces of the (gospel) harvest. However, when all the people who begged and received the best locations got tired out and came back to home-base the owner was ready to start one of the greatest and finest (gospel) harvests of all time. The owner was being rewarded for his generosity and patience. The harvest was always there right in front of him, but the timing was not until the others got worn out from thinking they had the best.

> **Response by Dreamer:** Right on target with the circumstances involved in their life's work and God's promises to them.
>
> **Special Note:** Notice that the dream involved the environment that the dreamer could relate to and actually enjoy.

Dream 2 – Get Some faith

The dreamer (she) is running out of the house and ready to go somewhere, but the only transportation is a bike. The problem is the bike is facing downhill, and the brakes are completely tied up with gray duct tape. She tries frantically to get the duct tape off the brakes so she can use the brakes. The more she tries to get the duct tape off the brakes, the more duct tape supernaturally gets added. It was so weird. She tried knives, scissors, cutters, and everything else, but the more she tried the more tape was added.

Interpretation 2:

The bike represents a new method of traveling for the dreamer. God is showing that the dreamer needs to learn different methods and not be so rigid. The brakes and duct tape represent a new time for the dreamer to start having more trust in God. In fact, God is asking the dreamer to get on board with His plan and have complete trust in the method of newness that God is selecting.

> **Response by Dreamer:** Right on target. Dreamer states that she is frightful of anything different, yet knows that God is calling her to do a new thing. Dreamer is literally afraid of traveling in airplanes and refuses to go places when asked via a method she is not comfortable with.
>
> **Special Note:** As simple as this dream appears, the dreamer did not understand. Fear is a powerful distracter from understanding God's will and purpose.

Dream 3 – A Young Lady's Dream of Variety

The dreamer (she) is shopping at a mall and there are all these fabulous items with colors that are vibrant in color. She is enjoying the experience, and then the worst thing possible happens; she is asked to try on a famous actress's dress. The problem is she hates the actress and the types of clothes the actress wears.

Interpretation 3

In the dream the colors and variety represent that God has seen her flare for creativity and variety and He wants to use this within the church. The trying on of the actress's dress is God's way of saying He wants this person to try on another of God's garments on and not to be so afraid and narrow-minded.

> *Response by Dreamer:* The interpretation is so true! I am a creative person and want to use my creativity for God. I am also doing something in life that I do not want to do. (In other words, a change of garments.)
>
> *Special Note:* As simple as this dream appears, the dreamer did not understand. Once again, fear is a powerful distracter from understanding God's will and purpose.

Dream 4 – A Strange and Funny Dream Indicates a Different Direction

The dreamer (he) is driving a car in a race with other cars. He is draped over the front seat, and he is operating the gas and brake with his hands. He is driving it through a winding road through a city. Somehow he ends up in this field and there is a woman who is trying to move this cow. Somehow the cow sits on the woman's head, and her head goes up the cow's back side so she starts kicking and screaming. When the cow gets up, the woman's head is covered in cow manure. He woke up laughing.

Interpretation 4:

It is apparent that God is making you aware that something in your life and surroundings are not operating in a normal sense. Because you are the driver, it is fair to say that there is a reminder to you that your life is operating in a backwards fashion; possibly going too fast and/or competing in things that are really not a fit for you; thus you are driving and competing in essence with your eyes closed and using the wrong body parts to compete. Your lifestyle or driving puts you in a place that is even weirder yet; a woman trying to also do things backwards, which ends up quite messy. All said and done, it is clear that the head (mind) of you and the lady are not settled and or focused on getting to where God has for you in a normal fashion. In a way it seems funny, but God is saying take your life more seriously.

Response by Dreamer:

That would explain a lot, lately. It sounds like I need to get back into seeking God's guidance and direction. To release my will and conform more to God's will in my life.

I do read the Bible and listen to Christian radio, but my prayer life needs definite improvement.

Special Notes: 1) God has a sense of humor and uses creative descriptions. 2) This is an ideal outcome of a dream interpretation; getting people back on course — God's course.

Dream 5 – Things Must be Viewed Differently at Times

The dreamer (she) is somewhere in a large multi-story building when she looks out the window. She saw a group was in 2 boats. Her friends were in one boat and the rest in the other. She said something about it to her husband that they were going without us. They were wearing heavy clothing and what looked to be life jackets. Suddenly the friend's wife fell out of the boat and floated downstream. She saw her spring out of the water backwards and land on her back on the land. "I knew she would be cold, so I started to look for towels. The closets where I was were mine from my house but I had a hard time finding towels. All my large beach towels except one were gone. By the time I got outside, Keith and Don had most of her clothes off but she was not naked. She didn't seem to be cold. The last thing before I woke up was seeing all this long hair on her chest and upper arms."

Interpretation 5:

It is apparent that the dream is in preparation for an upcoming conference that the dreamer and friends will be attending. The dream is showing that you have to view your friend's illness from a different viewpoint; thus the multi-story building where you're viewing them from. God is indicating things need to be viewed differently in this case. It also is representing that how you have and would normally handle the problem is different than how you will need to handle it; this is why there is the failure to find towels and realizing that she is not cold like you really think. The dream shows your friend has her own will, and there may be some abnormal things happening in her heart and mind, causing the problem.

Special Note: The friend's wife had been suffering with an un-described mental illness for years. The situation became frustrating for friends and family.

Dream 6 – Two Dreams Connected From the War

The dreamer (he) had two dreams sent in.

Dream A: The dreamer has been on his 4th military deployment; his second one in Iraq. He has had about 3 or 4 dreams since he was about 18. The last one he had about 4 years ago while coming back from Iraq. He was dreaming his wife and he had pulled into a parking lot where a bunch of kids were sitting in the parking lot loitering. "One of them told me to get my butt over here." He woke up screaming.

Dream B: The dreamer had just returned to Iraq and had a dream about his dog Spud. He loves the dog to death even though he is not very obedient. He was trying to chase someone down who was in his house. His wife and he had gotten on a bus and a kid was running desperately to catch the bus. He was so desperate that he started to vomit from running so hard to stop the bus. The kid told the driver to pull over. The weirdest thing was the bus was driving backwards. The kid spoke up and said "here" and gave him his dog Spud. He did not know why or how the kids got Spud or how he knew Spud was his dog. There was this other guy that was standing in the door of the bus, and he set Spud up next to him by the door of the bus. The other person was trying to move Spud closer to a seat so Spud could see his owner, but did not hand Spud over to the owner — the dreamer. After he moved Spud, Spud fell through a hole that was next to him that led underneath the bus. Keep in mind the bus is driving backwards. Spud was run over. The owner (dreamer) told the driver to stop again, as Spud was still trying to get back to the bus. The owner knew that Spud was going to die, even though Spud was not crushed. He went to him and picked him up, but did not see any blood. But the side of him was like cut open. He could see Spud dying in his arms, and his little heart and lungs were moving with his side that was cut open. Spud died after a few seconds, and he started telling Spud he was sorry and then he started crying and telling him he loves him.

Interpretation 6:

Both of your dreams are related. Primarily God is showing you how backwards things are becoming in America. Your first dream was given three times which is representative of how many times you have been deployed. It is also God's way of telling you to pay attention. It was God's way of saying in the grand scheme of life your three deployments have actually helped your family. The parking lot situation shows even though you prefer being here in America, for you personally this is not the safest situation. Even though you can't see it, the reality is God has protected your family through each of your deployments. Your second dream is God's way of saying that some bizarre things are and will be taking place in America (thus the bus driving backwards). The dog dying is only representing the fact that something and/or people will be injured in what may take place. Keep in mind that the dream fulfillment may be years away, but God is preparing you and others to get ready to see strange things happen.

> *Response by Dreamer:* I needed to hear that as our situation is strenuous and trying.
>
> **Special Notes:** 1) God uses what is close to us to represent things. In this case where a man may see life as a little less close and adorable, a dog or personal pet was used to show pain and suffering. 2). Note the irony of the dreams 3-4 times to match each deployment.

Dream 7 – Stay Focused on the Future, Not the Past

The dreamer (She) was traveling down a white hallway with a tall open doorway at the end. Outside is green grass and sky. Then a black spiraling smoke appears in front of her face along with lots of antique broaches with letters or words on them. The broaches appear very quickly from the top left to bottom right. Although she did her best to read the writing, it was going so fast that her mind was not able to comprehend the writing. She went through a few "pages" of text in this manner. Suddenly she appeared in a hospital bed, and two women came into the room which she knew to be angels. They sat next to her on the bed and started giving her gifts. The gifts started with an old broach that had blue on it. The only other things she remembered were a box of tiny caramels and a package of socks where one pair had already been worn on a much larger pair of feet. One of the angels also put a tiny round sticker on her left temple and said, "Here's $500 dollars." Then the angel handed her a clipboard to sign, and she half jokingly said, "I'm signing my life away, right?" But the dreamer signed it anyway, knowing it was serious. This whole time there was a question building in her, and she asked, "What do I do with my life?" The angel said, "Give us three days." Then the spiraling black smoke appeared again, and they were gone. A man came into her room to interpret her chart, and she said, "Good luck with that." She tried the socks on and laughed as she tried them on. Throughout all the gift giving, she was praising God and giving thanks. When she woke up, her first thought was, "Wow! That was a dream?" She was surprised to be sleeping.

Interpretation 7:

God is giving you a dream that includes various things that are being used to show you about your personality as well as His purpose and plan. God is indicating He has a beautiful plan, but it needs to be taken seriously. It includes a reminder of your tendency to always have multiple decisions and not coming to any final conclusions. More specifically:

- The white hallway and a tall open door represent God's Plan is good but it must be walked out. You are not to be distracted by simple things along the way (i.e. the walls, old broaches, and smoke which represent distractions). On the other side of the (single) door is God's peace and plan for you. The single hallway and door are a reminder to pick a single path, not multiple ones.

- The antique broaches represent old things (past things) in your life. The writing that you can't read is a way of God saying, "Don't try and figure out your past; it may not make any sense; look ahead."
- The hospital bed and two people as angels represent God saying, "Rest in me, and my angels will guide you and exchange your past with my future; thus the gifts and an exchange for a broach that is singular and not confusing."
- The two pair of socks represent a reminder that God is saying don't doubt His plan or judge the opportunities that don't appear normal.
- The single sticker represents that you are to get a single focus in your mind and be focused on what you decide to become serious over.
- The clipboard and signature represent that God desires you to take His plan seriously and ultimately make a decision.
- The black smoke represents the darkness in the geographical area where you live. The angels come and go through a dark smoke versus a clear light.
- The fact that you are asking what to do with your life and their response of "Give us three days," represents the need for you to trust God with one single decision, not multiple ones. Multiple decisions are confusing you.

All these things combined should allow you to see that God is also saying enjoy life and find humor in His call and plans. Don't do what has been natural via your past and talents.

Response by Dreamer:

Thank you!! I could interpret a bit of this, but your help makes so much sense and hits it on the head. If I could afford it, I'd hire a ton of people and implement lots of ideas. I have too many ideas. But I have to say I've been able to eliminate something big in my life this past week and realize something that is more important to me.

With much gratitude!!!

Dream 8 – A Small and Simple Dream

The dreamer is a young man who is going to Bible college to be a ministerial leader. He has great potential, yet struggles with leading people. The dreamer has a simple dream where he is actually SpongeBob SquarePants™ in real life.

Interpretation 8:

God is showing the dreamer that he is called to be a leader. However, because he continually jokes around about his leadership abilities and friends, people perceive him as a cartoon character versus a spiritual leader.

Response by Dreamer:

So true! Friends see me as a natural leader, but I am always joking versus leading them. Six months later God gave him another dream which is now saying he is a real leader.

Special Note: The young man responded and confessed his portrayal in the first dream, and it changes his behavior in college. Now he is on the right track for what God has called him to be.

Dream 9 – A Husband and Wife's Dream to Work Together

Wife's dream — The husband sends her on a missions trip, and the person she was traveling with tries to take advantage of her. She is completely shocked and befuddled and frustrated that her husband allowed her to go with a man they could not trust.

Husband's dream 2 days later — He and his wife are lying next to each other, and God is putting a girdle around the two of their hips and pouring brass or gold into the girdle. The girdle is hardened, and the husband and wife are joined at the hip so that everywhere they go they have to go together.

Interpretation 9:

God is giving instructions that the husband and wife are intended to work together in ministry and not go in separate directions. There is a warning that if they do not stay together and work together, a potential unfavorable event(s) may happen.

Response by Dreamers:

So true! A few years prior to the dreams, the couple knew God had been telling them to work together and stay together. These dreams are God's reminders of their call to work closely together in all ways.

Dream 10 — A Dream For No More Backsliding

The dreamer (he) was lying on the operating table having open-heart surgery for the second time. During the surgery something very strange happens. The doctors were all around his heart during the operation, but the blood of his body was gushing out of his legs. The doctors tried to stop the bleeding, but they could not stop the blood loss.

Interpretation 10:

The dream was a friendly reminder from God that your life was spared through open heart surgery. In similar fashion, you have a tendency to take the blood of Christ by accepting him into your heart, but then you pay no attention to your actions, and the price His blood paid escapes. God is warning you that you cannot take His blood lightly, as you never know when you will die. God wants you to accept His blood and keep His blood permanently.

Response by Dreamer:

That is very accurate of things as well as my situation.

Special Note: Once again God fulfills His purpose of dreams — to whisper into people's ears to seal up instruction to keep one's soul from hell.

As you have gathered from these sample dreams and the biblical dreams that were shared back in chapters 2-3; God takes dreams serious, and so should we. Dreams and visions are of such nature that we are encouraged in Scripture to record them. In Habakkuk 2:1-3, God tells Habakkuk to write the vision down as it will come to pass. In this passage God encourages us that visions will come to pass if they are His visions. Even though we do not know what the exact vision was, we do know that God told him to write it down and that it would come true.

> *I will stand my watch And set myself on the rampart, And watch to see what He will say to me, And what I will answer when I am corrected. Then the LORD answered me and said: "Write the vision And make it plain on tablets, That he may run who reads it. For the vision is yet for an appointed time; But at the end it will speak, and it will not lie. Though it tarries, wait for it; Because it will surely come, It will not tarry."* Habakkuk 2:1-3 (NKJV)

Chapter Seven

Summary

God Speaks While We Sleep
Do you believe what the Bible tells,
Or is it just another book?
Do you believe stone temples fell,
Or that they merely shook?
Do you believe in the gifts of the spirit,
Or are they just part of the story?
Are you too asleep to hear it;
Simply living in your own glory?
If so, you may think that's fine
But you may miss His divine design
Do you believe in the power of dreams,
Or blame it on last night's dinner?
Do you believe it's you God deems;
To sleep beside the winner?
If so don't doubt,
Dare to dream about:
Being on board with the Lord,
Heed His call, take his sword,
"God speaks while we sleep"
His words won't come cheap.
~ Adam Thoms

Dreams can be extremely potent and potentially life-changing when we take them seriously. As history has proven, men, women, and children have helped change the world by not just having dreams and visions, but by doing something with their dreams and visions. God has not started something new with dreams and visions; rather He has decided to increase them in the last days for many of the reasons mentioned in this book. Chuck Pierce made an excellent point when talking about dreams. He stated: *"If we are going to walk in the day and possess our inheritance then we need to learn how to rule the night."* This is absolutely true as we cannot allow chance or other influences to capture, twist, or delete our dreams merely by downplaying them or intentionally forgetting them. What we need to realize and appreciate is the absolute truth that our mind and thoughts are active at night. Therefore we should take serious what transpires when we are resting. Throughout this book the message has been conveyed that God chose dreams to elevate our minds and thoughts during times of change.

You and I have been blessed by a loving God that chose to use dreams to pull us to His level of understanding. His desire is to pull us up to His level, rather than come down to our level all the time. We need to learn and appreciate the many different ways in which God communicates. Throughout this book you have been challenged and educated in many of the ways in which dreams and visions have been utilized throughout history. If we as a people are called to love the Lord our God with all our heart, all our mind, and all our soul; then let's begin to make sure our entire mind is given to the Lord — even while we sleep.

> ***Jesus replied: "Love the Lord your God with all your heart and with all your soul and with all your mind."***
>
> *~ Matthew 22:37 (NIV)*

It is worth the time to read through the quotations on dreams listed below. Even though many of them have been listed throughout the book, they are intended to greatly encourage the reality of dreams and also challenge you to question what you have done about your own dreams. I believe in dreams as well as the potential of the dreams when a person has the sense to honor a dream by taking action to understand and potentially carry out the dream.

If you can imagine it you can create it. If you can dream it, you can become it.

~ William Arthur Ward

And God chose dreams because He foreknew that the day in which we live would be so perplexing that our minds would need to be recalibrated during the evening hours; thus part of His purpose for increasing dreams in the last days.

~ Michael L. Mathews

Go confidently in the direction of your dreams! Live the life you've imagined. As you simplify your life, the laws of the universe will be simpler.

~ Henry David Thoreau

I was not looking for my dreams to interpret my life, but rather for my life to interpret my dreams.

~ Susan Sontag

When God stated that all of creation would be waiting for the manifestations of the Sons of God, He specifically declared and proclaimed that all of His people would be used to reveal him — not just ministers — no one was excluded. It's time for the Church and ministers to release the sons and daughters of God.

~ Michael L. Mathews

We grow by dreams. All big men are dreamers. Some of us let dreams die, but others nourish and protect them, nurse them through the bad days ... to the sunshine and light which always come.

~ Woodrow Wilson

Dreams are like letters from God. Isn't it time you answered your mail?

~ Marie-Louise von Franz

And God chose dreams so that all of humanity could see the things that Daniel saw, including glimpses into our lives, societies, and the future.

~ Michael L. Mathews

If I want to see the things that Daniel saw, then I should do the things that Daniel did; including dreaming and living out my dreams.

~ Michael L. Mathews

Remember to always dream. More importantly, work hard to make those dreams come true and never give up.

~ Dr. Robert D. Ballard

If one advances confidently in the direction of his dreams, and endeavors to live the life which he has imagined, he will meet with a success unexpected in common hours.

~ Henry David Thoreau

And God chose dreams to allow the human mind to be expanded beyond the boundaries that our daily lives live within and fear during the daytime; He literally wants us to catch glimpses of His plans through us.

~ Michael L. Mathews

Dreams — a microscope through which we look at the hidden occurrences in our soul.

~ Erich Fromm

Dreams don't work unless you do.

~ John C. Maxwel

Dream lofty dreams, as you dream, so shall you become. Your vision is the promise of what you shall at last unveil.

~ John Ruskin

Dreams are illustrations from the book your soul is writing about you.

~ Marsha Norman

Sometimes, there's so much thrown at us in the workplace that it's hard to see through the smoke and mirrors. The only time we do that is when we dream. ~ Joshua Estrin,

Every challenge we face can be solved by a dream.

~ David Schwartz

And God chose to use dreams to allow the potential for no one to perish and for all of humanity to be without excuse; thus the increase in dreams in the last days.

~ Michael L. Mathews

Our truest life is when we are in dreams awake.

~ Henry David Thoreau

Society often forgives the criminal; it never forgives the dreamer.

~ Oscar Wilde

And God chose dreams to manifest himself through as He knew the man-made efforts of humanity would require divine intervention to allow individuals to see past man's feeble efforts to gain salvation.

~ Michael L. Mathews

We grow great by dreams. All big men are dreamers. They see things in the soft haze *of a spring day or in the red fire of a long winter's evening. Some of us let these great dreams die, but others nourish and protect them; nurse them through bad days till they bring them to the sunshine and light which comes always to those who sincerely hope that their dreams will come true.*

~ Woodrow Wilson

BIBLIOGRAPHY

Brynie, Faith Hickman. *101 Questions About Sleep And Dreams That Kept You Awake Nights — Until Now.* Minneapolis, MN: 21st Century Books, 2006.

Burke, Bob and Freeman, Chuck. *Give Me the Book!: The Story of Sam Cochran and Light For The Lost.* Oklahoma City, OK: Commonwealth Press, 2002.

Domhoff, G. William. *The Scientific Study of Dreams: Neural Networks, Cognitive Development, and Content Analysis.* Washington, DC: American Psychological Association, 2003.

Goll, James W., and Michal Ann. *Dream Language.* Shippensburg, PA: Destiny Image, Inc., 2006.

Goll, James W., *The Seer; The Prophetic Power of Visions, Dreams, and Open Heavens,* Shippensburg, PA: Destiny Image, INC., 2004

The International Association For the Study of Dreams: http://www.asdreams.org, accessed December 2008.

Pace-Schott, Edward F. *Sleep and Dreaming: Scientific Advances and Reconsiderations.* New York: Cambridge University Press, 2003.

Sheets Dutch, and Pierce Chuck, *Releasing the Prophetic Destiny of a Nation;* Shippensburg, PA: Destiny Image, INC., 2005

Rock, Andrea. *The Mind at Night: The New Science of How and Why We Dream.* New York, NY: Basic Books, 2005.

Taves, Ann. *Fits, Trances, and Visions: Experiencing Religion and Explaining Experiences from Wesley to James.* Princeton, NJ: Princeton University Press, 1999.

NOTES AND CONTACT INFORMATION

Note 1: The answer to how many "f's" are in the paragraph on page 18 is shown below.

Answer Key to the Number of "F's" Used in the Paragraph

The author o*f* this book is trying to *f*ocus our minds on the reality o*f* dreams and visions. He o*f* course is making some *f*abulous points o*f* interest; but I, o*f* course will have to read more be*f*ore I *f*orm an opinion *f*or mysel*f*. So *f*ar the book provides some good *f*ood *f*or thought. Without tipping o*ff* the author, I am starting to think this is one o*f* the best books I may have ever read.

The human mind generally processes the "f" in the word *of* as a "v." As stated, our minds do not process information as clearly as we think.

Note 2: The NET Bible is found at http://www.bible.org. The NET Bible project was commissioned to create a faithful Bible translation that could be placed on the internet, downloaded for free, and used around the world for ministry. The Bible is God's gift to humanity — it should be free. (Go to www.bible.org and download your free copy.) Permission is available for the NET Bible to be printed royalty-free for organizations like the The Gideons International who print and distribute Bibles for charity. The NET Bible (with all the translators' notes) has also been provided to Wycliffe Bible Translators to assist their field translators. The NET Bible Society is working with other groups and Bible societies to provide the NET Bible translators' notes to complement fresh translations in other languages. A Chinese translation team is currently at work on a new translation which incorporates the NET Bible translators' notes in Chinese, making them available to an additional 1.5 billion people. Parallel projects involving other languages are also in progress.

Contact Information

Michael L. Mathews can be contacted at Michael.mathews@focusonheaven.com

http://www.focusonheaven.com

IMPORTANT TAKE AWAYS BY READER

Another Book by Michael L. Mathews; What in Heaven and Hell is Happening
Can be ordered at Amazon.com, Authorhhouse.com, Barnes and Noble, and Amazon.com
ISBN: 978-1-4343-6125-7
Ministers Michael and Pamela Mathews

Michael L. Mathews holds degrees in both Biblical Studies and Technology Management. He has spent the last 20 years in a dual career as both a change management consultant as well as an ordained minister affiliated with numerous denominations and parachurch ministries. His background and hunger for God's truth and wisdom has allowed him to develop a systematic perspective that combines biblical history and future revelation to illustrate a modern-day understanding that enlightens truth for many.

Michael and Pam Mathews live in Ozark, Missouri. They have two wonderful daughters, Jessica and Tiffany

People around the world are experiencing dreams and visions at an alarming rate. *And God Chose Dreams* gives valuable insight on why dreams are increasing at this alarming rate. Learn why dreams have significant value for you, and why God chose this method to increase His communication to humanity in the changing times we live in.

> "And God chose dreams because He foreknew that the day in which we live would be so perplexing that our minds would need to be recalibrated during the evening hours –– thus part of His purpose for increasing dreams in the ever changing times we live in."

CPSIA information can be obtained at www.ICGtesting.com
227097LV00003B/1/P